Catastrophe or New Society?

A Latin American World Model

IDRC—064e

Catastrophe or New Society?

A Latin American World Model

Amílcar O. Herrera, Hugo D. Scolnik, Graciela Chichilnisky, Gilberto C. Gallopin, Jorge E. Hardoy, Diana Mosovich, Enrique Oteiza, Gilda L. de Romero Brest, Carlos E. Suárez, and Luis Talavera

(This work was performed at the Fundación Bariloche, Buenos Aires, Argentina, and was carried out with the aid of a grant from the International Development Research Centre, Ottawa, Canada. The views expressed are those of the authors and do not necessarily represent the views of the Fundación or the Centre.)

The Project Team

Amílcar O. Herrera (Director) *(Nonrenewable Resources, Pollution)*
Hugo D. Scolnik (Deputy Director) *(Demography, Mathematics)*
Graciela Chichilnisky *(Economics, Mathematics)*
Adolfo Chorni *(Health)*
Gilberto C. Gallopin *(Food, Pollution)*
Isabel Gómez *(Food)*
Cristian F. Gravenhorst (Assistant to the Director)
Jorge E. Hardoy *(Housing and Urbanization)*
Diana Mosovich *(Housing and Urbanization)*
Enrique Oteiza *(Education)*
Rafael Pastoriza *(Mathematics)*
Víctor H. Ponce *(Pollution)*
Gilda L. de Romero Brest *(Education)*
Juan V. Santiere *(Economics)*
Abraam Sonis *(Health)*
Juan V. Sourrouille *(Economics)*
Carlos E. Suárez *(Education)*
Luis Talavera *(Mathematics, Demography)*
Gregorio Weinberg (Editorial Adviser)

Consultant Committee
Helio Jaguaribe, Carlos A. Mallmann, Enrique Oteiza, Jorge Sábato, and Osvaldo Sunkel

Contents

Preface

The idea of building this model emerged at a meeting sponsored by the Club of Rome and the Instituto Universitario de Pesquisas de Rio de Janeiro in Rio de Janeiro in 1970. The meeting had been held to analyze and discuss "Model World III," which had been built by a group directed by Dennis L. Meadows at the Massachusetts Institute of Technology. Out of that meeting came the decision by the Latin Americans present to commit the Fundación Bariloche in Argentina to building a model based on the points of view expressed during the debate.

A committee composed of Carlos A. Mallmann, Jorge Sábato, Enrique Oteiza, Amílcar O. Herrera, Helio Jaguaribe, and Osvaldo Sunkel was established to outline the general aims of the project and to effect its implementation. The first four members of the committee then produced a document stating the hypotheses and variables to be used in the model by the end of 1971. At a later meeting attended by all committee members and some specialists, the general features of the model to be built were established.

Thus, the type of society — egalitarian, fully participatory, nonconsuming —, the concept of basic needs and its central role in the model, the use of a production function with substitution between capital and labour, the criteria with which the problems of natural resources, energy, and pollution would be treated, and the division of the world into regions, were defined.

As Project Director, I was entrusted with the task of selecting the specialists who would participate in it. In the final phase of the project, Dr Hugo Scolnik, who had been active in the direction of the project, was appointed Deputy Director, and was in charge of the project in my absence for a period of 7 months.

The list of project team members and their areas of responsibility does not fully reflect the actual participation of each in this work. The hypotheses and the basic philosophy of the model were the product of a long and hard collective task, and it is very difficult to differentiate the individual contributions.

Although the redaction of this monograph was under my direction (with the exception of the chapter on education, written by Gilda L. de Romero Brest), it also represents a collective effort. This monograph, which is a condensed version of the final report to be published in book form, was prepared on the basis of the technological reports made for each of the sectors and of the ideas that came out of the continuous discussion on the content and the meaning of the model. The first draft was reviewed by all the authors, and on the basis of their observations and suggestions the final version was prepared. Therefore, the text that follows represents the common thought of the authors, although it does not mean that each of them agrees with each idea presented. The partial divergencies, natural in a large group, were solved according to the opinion of the majority.

Amílcar O. Herrera
Director of the Project Team

Acknowledgments

The authors wish to thank:
- the United Nations agencies ILO, FAO, UNESCO, UNCTAD for their collaboration in providing essential data, as well as for the helpful discussions with their experts on several aspects of the model;
- the Club of Rome, for its initial support to perform the feasibility study of the model, and for its invitations to present the project at several of its meetings;
- the International Institute for Applied System Analysis (IIASA) of Vienna, for the organization of an international meeting in October 1974 to present the preliminary results of the model;
- the Centro Latinoamericano de Demografía de las Naciones Unidas (CELADE), Santiago de Chile, for its collaboration in the area of demography;
- the Science Policy Research Unit (SPRU) of the University of Sussex, for its constant encouragement;
- Honeywell Bull Argentina for its computational support;
- Xerox Argentina for the reproduction of the first draft of this book;
- the staff and personnel of the Fundación Bariloche, particularly the Computation Centre, for their constant collaboration;
- the collaboration in the Housing and Urbanization sector of the Centro de Estudios Urbanos y Regionales of the Instituto Di Tella (Buenos Aires); the Economic Commission for Latin America (ECLA, Santiago de Chile); and the Centre of Housing, Building and Planning (UN).

The authors also acknowledge the contribution of the following persons: Graciela Riquelme and María Teresa Fernandez (Education); Alberto Lapidus (Mineral Resources); Víctor Bravo (Energy); Carmen Arretz, Angel Fucaraccio, Alfredo Lattes, and Raul Singer (Demography); Marcos Kaplan (Sociopolitical Aspects).

They also thank Juan Sourrouille for his elaboration of the information now included in the data bank of the model and for his advice on the definition of the economic structure of the model.

Introduction

Any long-term forecast of the state of humanity is founded on a perception of the world that incorporates a system of values and a concrete ideology. An attempt to describe the current world structure and project into the future does not (as it is sometimes maintained) constitute an "objective" vision of reality, but necessarily implies the acceptance of an ideological position. For this reason, it is not justifiable to differentiate between extrapolative and normative models.

The model presented here is quite explicitly normative. It is not an attempt to discover what will happen if present trends continue but tries to indicate a way of reaching a final goal, the goal of a world liberated from underdevelopment and misery. It does not pretend to be "objective" in the sense of being value-free as generally understood. It portrays a conception of the world shared by its authors and to which they are deeply committed. On the other hand, it is objective in that it starts from a distilled but realistic view of the problems facing the world and seeks solutions based on the capacity for change and creativity that human societies have demonstrated so often in the past.

A goal of this magnitude cannot be totally encapsulated in a formalized structure. Thus the word "model" will be used in two ways: first, to refer to the concept of an "ideal" society, and secondly, to refer to a mathematical model.

The ideal society is a reaction against the school of thought, particularly prevalent in developed countries, that holds that the fundamental problems currently facing humanity are those of physical limits. According to this view, exponential increases in consumption and population will eventually exhaust the planet's natural resources, perhaps even in the near future. If the problems of depletion are avoided for the foreseeable future, growing pollution levels would then result in ecological collapse. The result is always the same: a major collapse with massive death rates and a decline in the standard of living to preindustrial levels.

The solutions proposed in some of the most influential circles in the developed countries can be summarized in a few words:

- the main problem is rapid population growth, especially in the Third World;
- if catastrophe is to be avoided, it is essential that this be contained;
- pollution control, the rational use of resources, etc., are only secondary measures.

The basic characteristic of this position is that it accepts, in a totally uncritical manner, the central values of society as it now is.

The stance of the present authors is radically different: it is argued that the major problems facing society are not physical but sociopolitical. These problems are based on the uneven distribution of power, both between

7

nations and within nations. The result is oppression and alienation, largely founded on exploitation. The deterioration of the physical environment is not an inevitable consequence of human progress, but the result of social organizations based largely on destructive values.

Our conceptual model of the "ideal" society is based on the premise that it is only through radical changes in the world's social and international organization that man can finally be freed from underdevelopment and oppression. What is proposed is a shift toward a society that is essentially socialist, based on equality and full participation of all its members in the decisions affecting them; consumption and economic growth are regulated in such a way as to attain a society that is intrinsically compatible with its environment.

It is not sufficient simply to describe an ideal society; it is necessary also to demonstrate its material viability. Thus we must start by showing beyond all reasonable doubt that, for the foreseeable future, the environment and its natural resources will not impose barriers of absolute physical limits on the attainment of such a society. Secondly, it must be demonstrated that different countries and regions of the world (particularly the poorest) could reach the goals we advocate within a reasonable period of time, starting from the current situation as regards the availability of capital, manpower, land, demographic trends, etc.

To attain the first objective — to demonstrate that absolute physical limits do not exist for the foreseeable future — an analysis was undertaken of the current situation in nonrenewable resources, energy, and pollution. A mathematical model was built to handle the second objective: establishing that all countries or regions of the world could move from their present situations to the postulated goals in a reasonable time. Thus the conceptual model is a proposal for a new society, and the mathematical model is the instrument through which its material viability is explored.

The mathematical model is based on the premise that, in the new society, the production system has the satisfaction of basic human needs as a main objective. These needs are nutrition, housing, education, and health, and their satisfaction is a prerequisite if a person is to take a full and active part in his social and cultural environment. This is a necessary condition for an egalitarian and free society but it is not in itself sufficient.

The mathematical model was centred around the satisfaction of basic needs. It is essentially an economic model or, more precisely, a model of the production system within which five sectors are differentiated: nutrition, education, housing, capital goods, and, finally, consumer goods and other services. This last sector comprises all that is not in the other four. The production function used permits substitution between capital and labour and reflects improvements in productivity brought about by technological progress.

One major characteristic of the model that distinguishes it from most others built so far is that population size is generated endogenously by a submodel that relates demographic variables to sociopolitical variables. This submodel permits the exploration of one of the basic hypotheses put forward in this study, namely, that *the only truly adequate way of controlling population growth is by improving basic living conditions*. Both the research conducted in constructing the demographic sector and the results of the computer runs (presented in Chapter 9) show this hypothesis to be essentially correct.

The main function of the economic system is to allocate capital and manpower between the five sectors so as to obtain an optimum distribution. The question then arises of how to define this optimum and how to attain it. After exhaustive research, it was decided to opt for the introduction of a mathematical mechanism that assigns resources to each of the sectors so that life expectancy at birth is maximized at each point during the run.

This criterion was chosen because the population model indicates that life expectancy is determined by, and is very sensitive to, the socioeconomic variables in the model. Consequently, instead of maximizing some economic indicator — GNP, for instance — as is usual in most works of this kind, the indicator selected truly reflects the general living conditions of a population.

The construction of a formalized model of the world necessarily entails constraints imposed by the methodology used. These constraints appear mainly in the form of simplifications of the real world. Some of these merit special attention here. The first problem posed in constructing a world model is the degree of political and geographical disaggregation. Should the world be treated as a single, homogeneous unit? If not, which units should be taken — nations, regions, continents? The solution used here is a compromise between two conflicting considerations. As mentioned above, the central objective is to define the time scales and conditions required for the adequate satisfaction of basic human needs. Naturally, the time scale depends upon the initial conditions in the country or region under investigation, and this clearly demands a first disaggregation into developed and developing countries to reflect their fundamental differences in the levels of material and economic well-being. The developed countries, as a group, are considerably more homogeneous than the developing countires, despite their differences in political and social organization, relative power, etc. For the purposes of this model, the former may be taken as a single bloc.

The developing countries, on the other hand, cover a broader spectrum. They range from countries with low population densities and of medium economic ranking to countries with large poverty-stricken populations. The model concentrates especially on the problems of the countries in the Third World, and so these receive more detailed treatment than do the more economically advanced nations.

The model stresses the importance of autarchy; what is proposed is to establish whether the various regions (or nations) can attain the specified goals using, in the main, their own resources. Bearing in mind disparities in land area and in endowments of different countries, it is obvious that regional economic complementarity plays an essential role in autonomous development. This applies not only to the complementary elements within each country but also, in the wider context, to the pooling of resources by countries with similar problems, a process that is aided by geographic proximity.

To fulfill these two requirements — relative uniformity of initial economic conditions, and geographic proximity — it was decided to divide the developing countries into three continents: Latin America, Africa, and Asia.

Even within these blocs, great disparities can be found. Perhaps the ideal solution would have been to disaggregate them into yet more homogeneous regions, but operational requirements precluded this. Firstly, information about the indicators used is frequently scarce and untrustworthy in the

9

underdeveloped countries. To disaggregate further would have entailed introducing high levels of uncertainty in much of the data. Secondly, greater disaggregation, rather than contributing significantly to the central objectives of the model, would have complicated it and made it unmanageable.

Another simplification, perhaps of greater importance, is that political and social diversities between countries within a group are not taken into account. Thus no distinction is drawn between capitalist and socialist countries, be they industrialized or developing.

This is justified by the objective of the model, which is to attempt to demonstrate the material feasibility of the proposed new society. The results presented in Chapter 9 are based on the assumption that, by 1980, policies that tend toward the desired society will begin to be implemented. Thus the current differences in political systems cease to be significant from then onward.

This study does not explore the mechanism through which the world may reach the proposed objectives. This is largely because, as history shows, it is very difficult to predict the processes through which social change will take place; in any case, this was not the aim of the exercise.

The main objective is to demonstrate that it is possible to liberate society from underdevelopment, oppression, and misery. Whether this actually occurs or not will depend upon the will and actions of men. If the model contributes to mobilizing this will in the proposed direction, it will have fulfilled the objective of the authors.

Finally, a brief clarification should be given of some of the terms used in the study. The expressions "underdeveloped countries," "developed countries," and "Third World" are used by the authors with different meanings and in different contexts and so, in using them, there is the risk that they will be interpreted in a way that has little to do with the intentions of the authors. It should therefore be said that these expressions are used for lack of better alternatives and with a purely descriptive intention.

Chapter 1

The Current World

Misery and Overconsumption

The most outstanding feature of the world today is the fact that nearly two-thirds of humanity live in a state of poverty and misery, while the remaining minority is beginning to feel the effects of overconsumption resulting from uncontrolled economic growth that destroys the natural and human environment. This inequality, which has been increasing, is most clearly manifested in the present division of the world into developed and underdeveloped countries; it is not, however, totally characterized by rigid political boundaries. Privileged minorities in the countries of the Third World have consumption rates that are equivalent to those of the upper classes in developed countries, while a considerable proportion of the population in the underdeveloped countries have not yet fully satisfied their most basic material and cultural needs.

In the maps in Fig. 2–6 the extent of the unequal distribution of wealth between nations is clearly shown in terms of its effects on the socioeconomic factors that most directly influence standard of living. On all the maps, the area of the countries is proportional to their populations to indicate clearly the proportion of the world population affected by different deficiencies.

Figure 2 shows the distribution of food in the world, expressed in average consumption of calories and protein per person per day.

Figure 3 uses a combined index to indicate the housing situation. This index includes factors representing each of the following: crowding (percentage of the population having two or more persons per room); percentage of the population without running water within a radius of 100 metres of their houses; percentage of the population without electricity; percentage of the population without toilets; number of houses built per 1000 inhabitants per year; and life expectancy at birth. This last factor is used to estimate the others where there is no published data on them. The maximum value for each factor is 10, so that the maximum value of the combined index is 60.

Figure 4 indicates the level of education expressed as the percentage of illiterate people over the age of 15.

Figure 5 shows life expectancy values at birth. This is the indicator most widely used to characterize the state of health of a population.

Energy consumption per capita is represented in Fig. 6. Although this indicator is useful in that it contributes a general idea of the well-being of a society, it is liable to misinterpretation if considered in isolation. In general it

FIGURE 1

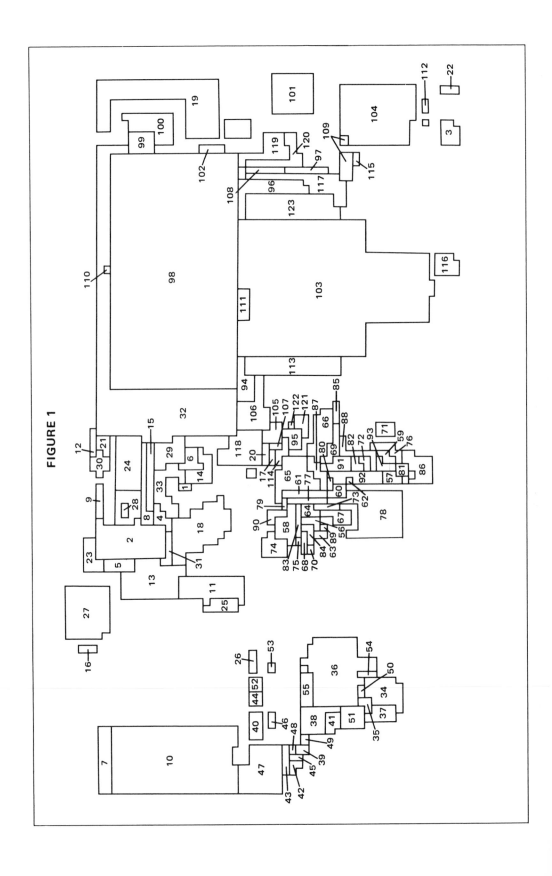

Fig. 1. The world, in which the area of a country is drawn in proportion to its population. The numbers coincide with the following countries:

Region 1
1 Albania
2 German Federal Republic
3 Australia
4 Austria
5 Belgium
6 Bulgaria
7 Canada
8 Czechoslovakia
9 Denmark
10 USA
11 Spain
12 Finland
13 France
14 Greece
15 Hungary
16 Ireland
17 Israel
18 Italy
19 Japan
20 Lebanon
21 Norway
22 New Zealand
23 Low Countries
24 Poland
25 Portugal
26 Puerto Rico
27 United Kingdom
28 German Democratic Republic
29 Rumania
30 Sweden
31 Switzerland
32 USSR
33 Yugoslavia

Region 2
34 Argentina
35 Bolivia
36 Brazil
37 Chile
38 Colombia
39 Costa Rica
40 Cuba
41 Ecuador
42 El Salvador
43 Guatemala
44 Haiti
45 Honduras
46 Jamaica
47 Mexico
48 Nicaragua
49 Panama
50 Paraguay
51 Peru
52 Dominican Republic
53 Trinidad and Tobago
54 Uruguay
55 Venezuela

Region 3
56 Upper Volta
57 Angola
58 Algeria
59 Burundi
60 Cameroons
61 Chad
62 Congo
63 Ivory Coast
64 Dahomey
65 Egypt
66 Ethiopia
67 Ghana
68 Guinea
69 Kenya
70 Liberia
71 Madagascar
72 Malawi
73 Mali
74 Morocco
75 Mauritania
76 Mozambique
77 Niger
78 Nigeria
79 Libya
80 Central African Republic
81 Rhodesia
82 Rwanda
83 Senegal
84 Sierra Leone
85 Somalia
86 South Africa
87 Sudan
88 Tanzania
89 Togo
90 Tunis
91 Uganda
92 Zaire
93 Zambia

Region 4
94 Afghanistan
95 Saudi Arabia
96 Burma
97 Cambodia
98 People's Republic of China
99 Korea, North
100 Korea, South
101 Philippines
102 Hong Kong
103 India
104 Indonesia
105 Iraq
106 Iran
107 Jordan
108 Laos
109 Malaysia
110 Mongolia
111 Nepal
112 New Guinea
113 Pakistan
114 Syria
115 Singapore
116 Sri Lanka
117 Thailand
118 Turkey
119 Vietnam, North
120 Vietnam, South
121 Yemen
122 Yemen, Democratic
123 Bangladesh

13

FIGURE 2

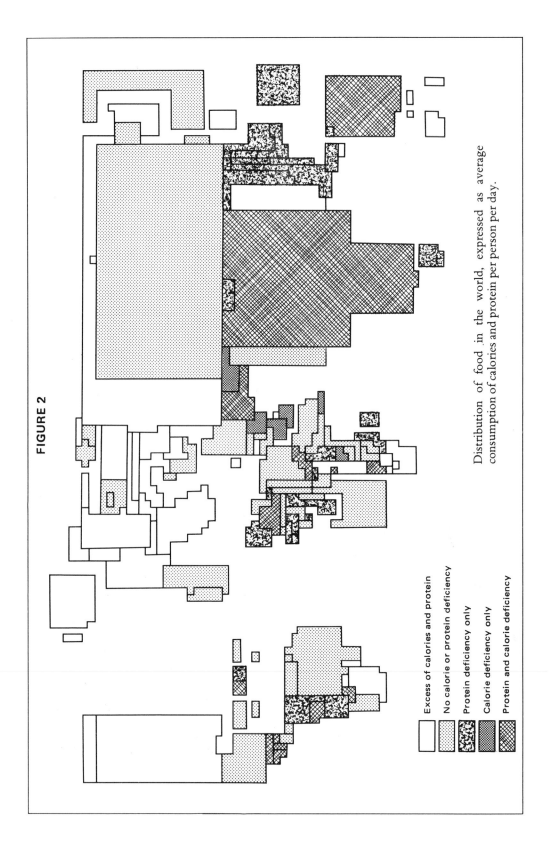

Distribution of food in the world, expressed as average consumption of calories and protein per person per day.

Excess of calories and protein

No calorie or protein deficiency

Protein deficiency only

Calorie deficiency only

Protein and calorie deficiency

FIGURE 3

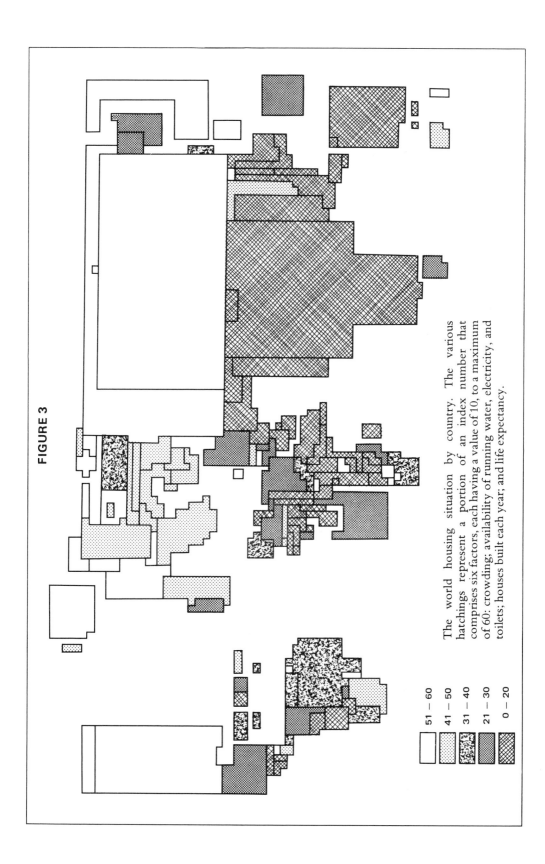

The world housing situation by country. The various hatchings represent a portion of an index number that comprises six factors, each having a value of 10, to a maximum of 60: crowding; availability of running water, electricity, and toilets; houses built each year; and life expectancy.

51 — 60
41 — 50
31 — 40
21 — 30
0 — 20

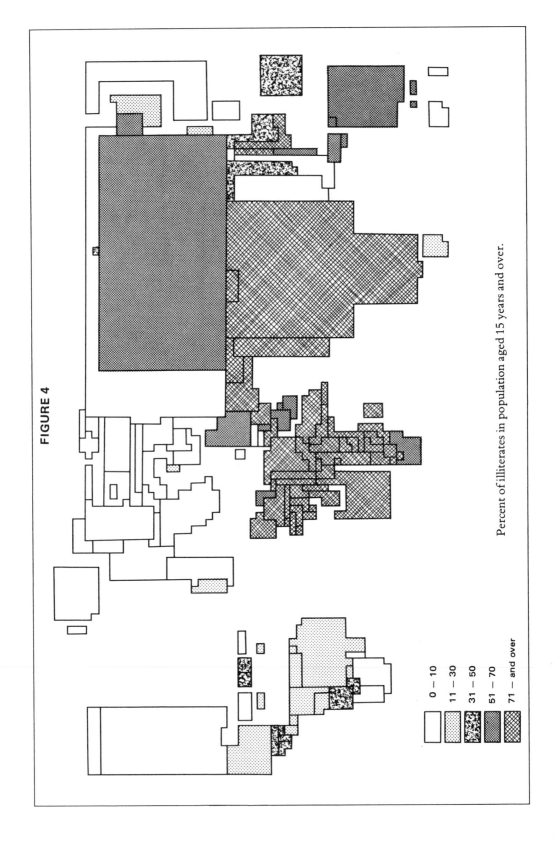

FIGURE 4

Percent of illiterates in population aged 15 years and over.

0 — 10
11 — 30
31 — 50
51 — 70
71 — and over

FIGURE 5

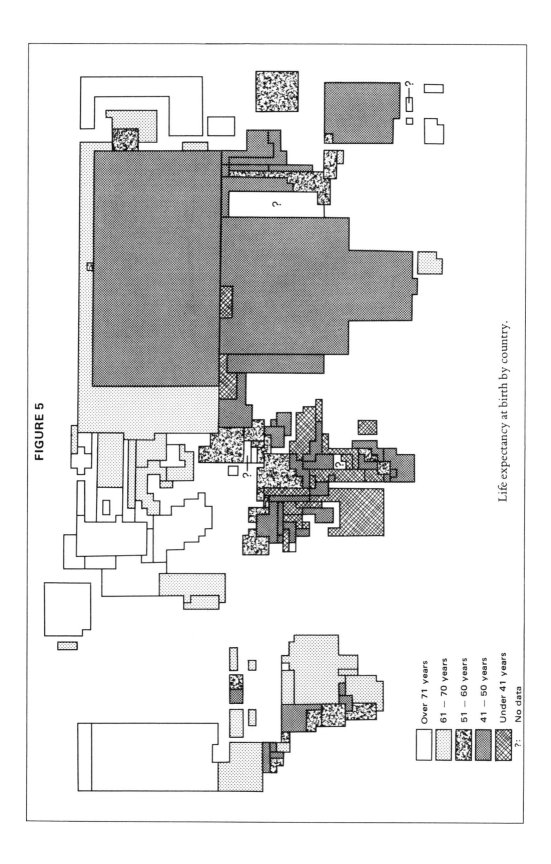

Life expectancy at birth by country.

Over 71 years
61 — 70 years
51 — 60 years
41 — 50 years
Under 41 years
?: No data

FIGURE 6

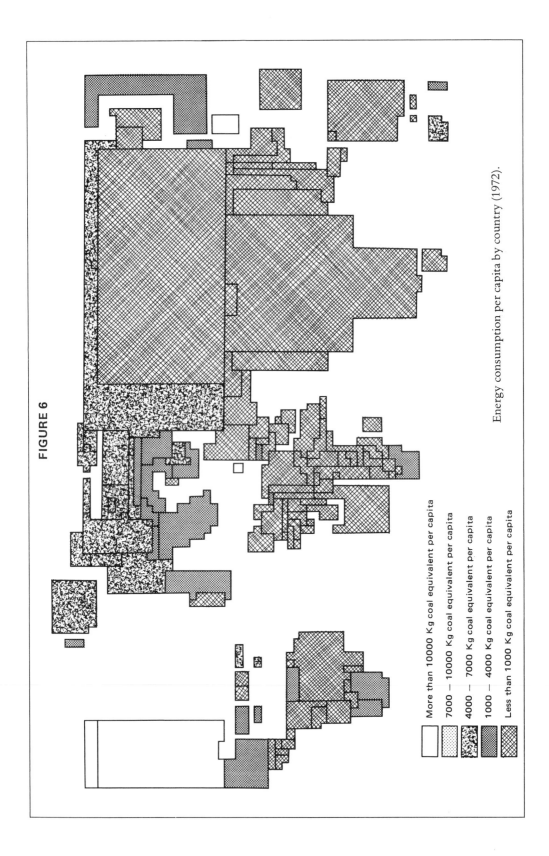

Energy consumption per capita by country (1972).

More than 10000 Kg coal equivalent per capita

7000 — 10000 Kg coal equivalent per capita

4000 — 7000 Kg coal equivalent per capita

1000 — 4000 Kg coal equivalent per capita

Less than 1000 Kg coal equivalent per capita

may only be used as a measure of the level of industrialization, which cannot necessarily be taken to represent a certain standard of living.

In all the maps, the darkest shading represents the areas with the greatest need. As can be seen, there are regions where all the indicators take their minimum values; almost two-thirds of the world population are to be found in these regions. The presence of misery and underdevelopment is the main characteristic of these Third World countries.

The Sociopolitical Framework

The sociopolitical systems operating in this unjust and unequal world are many, but all are variations on two broad models: the capitalist and the socialist systems. The first is without doubt the dominant system, and the one that, to varying degrees, operates in most underdeveloped countries. The second, although more recent and less widespread, is expanding, and would seem to be the only valid alternative to the capitalist system to date.

It is obviously impossible here to attempt an analysis of the different variations within each model. We will only attempt to outline some of their more essential features.

The Capitalist Model — Whatever its form, capitalism is based on property, initiative, and private profit, and gives rise to societies based on class structures in which there is inequality, dominance, and exploitation.

Some of the features of the system designed to maximize efficiency and productivity, such as the extreme division and specialization of labour, are more typical of an industrial society than of capitalism itself. Even so, the goal of personal gain, which has led to the commercialization of almost all aspects of society, ensures that these features develop to their fullest extent under capitalism.

When economic growth, as measured by the total production of material goods, becomes an objective in itself, it is increasingly accompanied by a tendency toward the subordination of all other aspects of social life; this concept of "progress" tends to ignore the specificity of cultures and all qualitative features of life that cannot be expressed in economic terms. At the level of the individual, the personality is manipulated, particularly through education, the mass media, and information.

It is clear that in developed countries — in spite of "pockets of poverty" and the persistence of social inequality — capitalism has attained high levels of material well-being for most of the population. But the prevalence of inequality, and the use of persuasion and manipulation as means of social control, leads to alienation, to an extent at least as great as when this is caused by direct compulsion or repression.

Capitalism in underdeveloped countries, although having, in varying degrees, the same general characteristics as in the industrialized countries, also has some particularities that are largely due to the position of these countries in the international power structure. Underdevelopment is not merely the first stage toward development but represents a different structural situation, largely generated and conditioned by the existence and evolution of developed societies. During the process of colonial expansion, and particularly as a result of the industrial revolution, the countries of the Third World were incorporated into the international capitalist system as peripheral, dependent economies, essentially exporters of raw materials and

19

importers of manufactured goods originating from the great industrial centres. The structure was based on the alliance between local beneficiaries (such as landowners and importers and exporters, who always held political and economic power, directly or indirectly, in the Third World) and the international centres of world power.

This type of dependent and unequal capitalist development in underdeveloped countries brought with it, among other things, a clear division between the urban and rural sectors. The former (containing from 10 to over 40% of the population) have standards of living and consumption patterns comparable to those of the developed countries, whereas the rural sector lives in conditions of extreme poverty. The relationship between the urban and rural sectors is very similar to that which arose between developed and underdeveloped countries.

In recent decades, a new form of dependency has arisen. One of the reasons for this is that, in the new international context, it is difficult to impose the direct political and military dominance that was the most outstanding feature of imperialism in the last century. The new instrument of domination, which is more subtle although no less effective, is the scientific and technological superiority of developed countries. This superiority is causing a new international division of labour, in which the great powers have a virtual monopoly over the most advanced techniques and production processes; dependent countries have to concentrate on other sectors of production that because of their low profitability, are not compatible with the high standards of living of the developed countries.

The intention is not to attribute sole responsibility for the situation of the Third World to the great powers, nor to the rest of the developed world; it is clear that Third World countries share a specific set of problems that are determined, in the last analysis, by the relationships between structures and processes of domination and exploitation (both internally and externally) and by the conflicts that arise from this double dynamic of underdevelopment.

The Socialist Model — The main form of this model, as developed by Marx, and his followers, proposes the abolition of private ownership of the means of production and the construction of a classless society where there is no domination, exploitation, or inequality. The original concept denies the very possibility of national socialisms; what is proposed is the construction of a new world order based on solidarity and on an international division of labour that excludes exploitation or dominance.

To judge the extent to which socialist projects have measured up to the original ideal, two important points should be borne in mind: first, the revolutionary road has not opened up in developed countries (as foreseen in the theory) but in backward, predominantly agricultural societies with incipient industrialization; secondly, the underdeveloped countries have no previous experience of popular participation and, in the cases of the Soviet Union and the People's Republic of China (PRC) had a long tradition of strongly autocratic central government.

The combination of these two historic factors — the need for rapid growth and industrialization that favours, and in some ways requires, a firm, centralized direction; and the lack of experience of the population in participation — led to the appearance of party and state bureaucracies that were transformed into strongly centralized power structures, authoritative and strictly hierarchical. This power elite, which sets the social roles, goals, and status with almost no popular participation, reintroduces social differences that are no longer based on personal accumulation of wealth but on the degree of membership or access to the minority that holds political power. Another consequence of this concentration and form of exercising power is the imposition of cultural patterns based on a narrow and dogmatic interpretation of the dominant ideology, virtually negating any right to cultural diversity.

This outline obviously does not apply equally to all socialist regimes. It is illustrated most clearly by the Stalinist period in the Soviet Union, a country that still retains many of the characteristics of that period, although to a lesser extent. In the PRC, Cuba, and Yugoslavia, popular participation is much greater; however, in these countries, participation would seem to depend more on the degree of permissiveness of the groups in government than on any real access of the masses to the institutional mechanisms of power and social control.

It is clear, therefore, that the socialist states have not yet achieved the creation of societies where freedom, equality, and justice are realized. From this point of view, they are still far from having achieved their original ideal.

Despite these deficiencies, socialist regimes have shown achievements of real historic significance. First, through the socialization of the means of production, they have suppressed one of the basic structures on which social inequality is based. Secondly, they have shown how an effort to satisfy the basic needs of the majority of the population can raise the general standard of living of some of the most backward nations in the world at an almost unprecedented rate.

The above analysis, which is clearly very general, does not try to deny positive values to both models. Bourgeois capitalism, which resulted from the political and technical revolutions of the 16th and 19th centuries, was one of the most dynamic movements in history and opened an era of human development without precedent. Socialist revolutions, for their part, put an end to some of the most retrograde regimes in the modern world, and indicated the way to a new option for overcoming the contradictions within capitalism. In both cases, the ideal of overcoming historical constraints is one of the main objectives. Another important central element shared by both systems is the concept of history as an open-ended process, whose direction depends, in the last analysis, on the will and actions of man.

Chapter 2

A World For All

A Critique of Contemporary Society

The atmosphere of defeatism and despair alluded to in the Introduction, and which is paradoxically most prevalent in the rich countries, is accompanied by other changes in attitudes. As in many previous historical periods, signs of decadence in the social structure are leading to the appearance of elements that shape the possibility for a new order. Apathy and frustration are being translated into the rejection of the present social and international order, which is seen as unjust and oppressive, and into the will to conceive and build an alternative society, even if this alternative society is still described only in the most general terms.

Although this trend, which is still new, appears in both rich and poor countries, it has been debated most in the latter. The reasons for this are clear: being the main victims of the system, the underdeveloped countries are in a situation that forces them to explore all possible options. It is in these countries that the need for change in the social and international organization is most strongly felt because of the way in which the present situation hampers the full development of humanity.

Although there is less of this critical questioning in the developed countries, it is found among sections of the young and among intellectuals. In rich societies, alienation has superseded direct oppression and misery as the major problem. There is a convergence between the position of the Third World and that of the industrialized countries: an analysis of the underlying cause of alienation shows it to be essentially the same as that of exploitation and misery. This is the existence of a system of social and international organization that is directed toward competitive accumulation of wealth, lacking any spirit of international harmony and goodwill, and which, by reducing people to mere tools of production, precludes any possibility of integrated human development.

The main result of this nonconformist and critical attitude is that, for the first time since the European powers began their colonial expansion, a movement has appeared that truly begins to unite broad sectors in both the developed and developing countries around common aspirations and objectives. This is without doubt the most important indication we can find that there is a feeling of international solidarity forming in the world that can be used to bring about a new social order.

What are the central elements of the new society that is being advocated? Because we are not so much attempting to outline a concrete plan, but rather contributing to a long and difficult gestation process, we do not attempt to give definitive answers to this question. However, some implicit elements can already be identified, and a coherent program of change can be built around them.

In the first place, there is the awareness that the current obstacles to harmonious development are essentially sociopolitical, and that they determine the current distribution of power at both the global and national levels. Secondly, there is the growing understanding that the current crisis is universal because, for the first time in history, technological and political forces tend to integrate the world into a single unit. In particular, the destiny of the Third World is intimately linked to that of the rest of humanity, and, if its situation continues to deteriorate, there will inevitably be catastrophic consequences for the privileged countries.

Taken in isolation, these elements provide only a partial view of reality. They acquire their full significance when placed in the context of some basic values that, although rooted in history, have been revitalized by the current desire for change. Two of these values are central: the growing acceptance of the fundamental equality of man, and the concept of history as an open-ended process, whose direction depends in the final analysis on the desires and actions of men. The first constitutes the only valid basis for building a truly harmonious world; the second is a prerequisite for attaining this world.

The Proposed Society

Starting with the basic elements derived from the above critique, the following pages present an outline of a possible world and attempt to describe a new course for the development of mankind. The proposal is based on the following general premises:

(a) Some models in vogue (be they mathematical or otherwise) predict that, if current trends continue, the not-too-distant future will see a catastrophe on a world scale.

The catastrophe predicted is already a reality for the majority of mankind. Hunger, illiteracy, premature death, inadequate housing — in other words, miserable living conditions — form the common destiny shared by the majority of the inhabitants of underdeveloped countries.

To correct this situation must be the top priority of any vision of the world and its future.

(b) The underdeveloped countries cannot advance by retracing the steps followed in the past by the now developed countries: this is not only because of the historic improbability of such a retracing being feasible, given the current sociopolitical conditions, but (and more importantly) because it is not desirable. It would imply repeating those errors that have led to the current situation of wasteful and irrational consumption and accelerated social deterioration of the environment — both stemming principally from consumption by developed nations and by privileged minorities in developing countries — that are the result of a system of values that is largely destructive. The solution to these problems cannot be centred around a few simple modifications to the present pattern, but must be based on the creation of a society that is intrinsically compatible with its environment.

(c) Any policy of protection of the environment, including a reduction in the consumption of natural resources, will be difficult to implement effectively on a world scale until each and every human being has attained an acceptable standard of living. It would be absurd to ask the people of the vast, poor regions of the world — most of whom exist at or near

24

subsistence levels — to worry about the distant future, given their present meagre levels of consumption.

(d) The privileged sections of mankind, and especially those in developed countries, should reduce their rate of economic growth to alleviate the pressure on natural resources and the environment, as well as to counteract the alienation effects of excessive consumption. Part of the economic surplus of these countries should be channeled into helping the countries of the Third World overcome their current stagnation, which is largely the result of the exploitation to which they were (and, indeed, still largely are) subjected.

In keeping with the above, a model of a society organized around three basic assumptions is put forward. The central features of these assumptions refer to development and social organization. A detailed description of this society is not attempted. This is because, when looked at in its full complexity, any historical process is essentially original; and, although novel solutions to problems are found, previously unforseen problems also arise, and these influence the social evolution. Additionally, the ultimate basic objectives may be fundamentally the same, but our knowledge of cultural diversity suggests that each group will probably follow its own route.

Thus, without attempting a detailed description, the following sketch indicates some of the more general characteristics of the nucleus around which a coherent and viable new world society could be shaped.

(i) The final goal is *an egalitarian society, at both the national and international levels*. Its basic principle is the recognition that each human being, simply because of his existence, has inalienable rights regarding the satisfaction of basic needs — nutrition, housing, health, education — that are essential for complete and active incorporation into his culture.

These needs are taken to be basic because, unless each one of them is satisfied, it is impossible to participate actively and with dignity in the human universe. These needs are invariable in that they are common to all members of the species, regardless of culture, origin, race, sex, etc.

(ii) The society proposed in the model is *not a consumer society; production is determined by social needs and not by profit*. One of its essential features is that consumption is not an end in itself.

Obviously, it is very difficult to establish what "social needs" are in terms of consumption, over and above those that we have called basic needs. Historically, they have changed with each society and through time. New needs are continually generated by the evolution of cultures, by different forms of social organization, and by technological change. In judging which needs are "legitimate," there is a risk of injecting a large dose of subjectivity.

For this reason, instead of trying to establish some quantitative criterion for identifying and assessing these needs, it is more important to try and give some idea of which should be the mechanisms for establishing the legitimacy of needs in the new society. Participation would play a central role here.

Although we assume the free expression of needs and aspirations of each person in the proposed society, decisions are channeled through the mechanism of collective action. This can be developed by starting with those places where individual participation is most feasible, such as in production units of goods and services. Depending upon their significance for the community, issues are discussed, and decisions taken, at different levels in the social and political organization.

The result of this procedure will be the creation of new criteria for deriving a hierarchy of needs that is relevant not only to the individual but also to the establishment of the new social order.

(*iii*) *Ownership and the use of property and means of production* play a key role in every society. What is the role of property in the world described in the model?

It is clear that, in our context, the concept of property loses much of its meaning. The private ownership of land and the means of production do not exist, but on the other hand, neither does the state own them as is currently the case in many centrally planned economies.

The present-day concept of private ownership of the means of production should be replaced by the more universal concepts of the *use* and *management* of the means of production. How to manage them would be decided and organized through the same discussion processes that would regulate all the other social activities. Depending on the nature and importance of the activity, its management would be the responsibility of production units, ad hoc committees, and/or communes of the state.

Within this conceptual framework, many different forms of management and administration of property will be found — depending on traditions, cultural features, and social organization — that will eliminate property as a means of achieving power or personal privileges.

The World Order

The application of the "ideal" model to a growing number of regions or countries would provide the basic conditions needed for the creation of a harmonious world order, capable of providing justice, overall well-being, and democracy, and of suppressing the roots of war.

The ultimate objective would be the emergence of some form of organization on a world scale that, although respecting the freedom and individuality of nation states, would promote gradual integration into a cosmopolitan world society, a world reflecting a united human consciousness. No doubt, this emergence will be a long and difficult process, but any hope of facing the future problems of the world in a rational manner must be based on its success.

Chapter 3

The Physical Limits to Development

The possibility of a world society in which all human beings attain adequate living standards (as outlined in the previous chapter) is denied implicitly (and sometimes explicitly) with the argument of insuperable physical limits. This argument is especially prevalent in developed countries. The limits are those imposed by the depletion of natural resources, expected in the not-too-distant future, and by the lethal effects of growing pollution. Linked with these is the question of whether it will be possible to produce energy in the quantities required by increased populations with increased per capita levels of consumptions.

What foundation is there for the view that physical limits will create unsurmountable obstacles for development? What follows is an attempt to answer that question.

Nonrenewable Resources

To understand the problem of nonrenewable resources, the concepts of mineral reserves and resources must be clarified, especially since there has been confusion in the literature regarding these concepts.

Mineral Reserves and Resources — The sources from which man obtains the raw materials for industry include the earth's crust, the seas, and the atmosphere. So far, most of the minerals that man has needed have been extracted from the earth's crust. Although its thickness varies from 32 to 40 kilometres, it has been rare for mining operations to penetrate beyond 2000–3000 metres. Even taking just this superficial layer, the earth's crust contains, in absolute terms, practically inexhaustible *resources* of virtually all the metals and minerals required by man, although most of this is distributed evenly through the crust and is hence found in low concentrations. The cost of extracting low-grade deposits exceeds their economic and social value, and therefore, with current technology, they cannot be considered to be exploitable.

Those deposits that are currently considered to be exploitable are found in geological forms called "ore bodies" and comprise high concentrations of certain elements or minerals. For such a concentration to be considered an ore, *it must be possible to extract one or more metals or minerals from it economically*.

This definition seems to offer a relatively simple method of determining whether the concentration of a metal or mineral deposit makes it an ore body or not. However, this simplicity is an illusion; the factors that determine the economic viability of exploitation are many and varied.

Most individual ore bodies are evaluated with a view to more-or-less immediate exploitation. When an attempt is made to estimate the mineral

27

resources of a region, the problem is different. The criterion generally adopted in this type of evaluation is to classify as a *reserve* any deposit exploitable under current economic and technological conditions, or those expected to prevail in the near future. The anticipation of these future conditions is clearly somewhat arbitrary and subjective, and estimates of the mineral wealth of a given region may vary widely from one author to another.

To summarize, it can be said that the wealth of a mineralized area or region cannot be expressed in absolute, unconditional terms, but only in relation to a specified economic and technological situation. Even then, there will be a large margin of error.

Reserves — What appears in statistics as the mineral reserves of a country comprises, firstly, the known reserves *declared* by companies and, secondly, estimates based on the best theory and information available. Almost all of this information is derived from mineralized areas that, if they have not already been mined, have at least already been explored. Therefore, all estimates of potential reserves are the result of geological extrapolations from mineral areas *already known*. In other words, these estimates of potential future discoveries are a function of the exploitable reserves that have been found in the past and, because there is no incentive to explore unless there is a market for the minerals found, these past discoveries have been a function of demand *in the production system*.

This argument sheds light on the figures given in published statistics on, for instance, the mineral reserves of a particular country or of the world as a whole. In no way are such estimates of reserves attempts to express the total mineral wealth of the region considered; they are the result of discoveries made up to that moment and made while searching for deposits exploitable with current technology (or that of the immediate future). For this reason, mineral inventories (and especially those of known reserves) are out-of-date from the moment they are published. Thus it is clear that the term "reserve" is dependent upon the economic and technological conditions prevailing at the time of the evaluation. In the future, different combinations of these two conditions will lead to very different pictures of the reserve position, both regarding types of ores and their quantities.

This can be illustrated from recent history. For most mineral raw materials, consumption so far this century has been greater than the reserves known in 1900. The reserves known then have not only been exhausted, but for nearly all important minerals the reserves known now are much greater than they were then. Thus it is erroneous to think of mineral resources as a fixed and unchangeable stock that might, at most, vary in quantity, as is frequently done in forecasts of catastrophe.

The concept of reserves is essentially dynamic. The terms used to define mineral reserves — quantity, type, concentration, etc. — should be viewed as variables that can change over time and with new technology and economic conditions.

Consequently, theoretical hypotheses of scarcity, as traditionally put forward in economics, cannot now be applied to mineral resources. It cannot be assumed a priori that scarcity existed in the past, or is likely to occur in the future. The problem of whether there are signs of scarcity in minerals can only be solved through a study of the historical evidence available.

The most significant historical evidence is that of production costs. These have been investigated by Barnett and Morse[1] in an analysis of the hypotheses of growing scarcity of natural resources. Their data refer to the USA but their conclusions are generally valid because the mining industry uses practically the same technology throughout the world.

Figure 7(a) from their book shows the development of mineral production in the USA between 1870 and 1960 and changes in the capital and labour inputs. Figure 7(b) shows that from 1890 production costs in terms in capital and labour inputs have steadily declined.

This analysis goes up to 1960 as the authors had no data available on costs after that year, but the type of ore bodies being exploited has not varied in the last decade, and the technology in use is essentially unchanged. In consequence, the cost of production (in terms of physical inputs) has not varied. It is probable that prices will increase as a consequence of action taken by those developing countries that are exploiters, so as to protect their position. This would result in a transfer of economic resources from rich to poor countries.

In summary, an analysis of the historical situation indicates that, far from there having been signs of increased scarcity of raw materials, the actual costs to society have been declining.

Mineral Availability in the Future

What is the probability that a scarcity of raw materials could occur in the future? A full answer to this requires a determination (even if crude) of the total quantities of accessible reserves.

Given that reserves must be defined in relation to technology and price, it is clearly impossible to establish the ultimate total quantity for any nonrenewable resource. To do this, information would be required that is currently unobtainable. First, a full and detailed knowledge of the physical and chemical characteristics of that part of the earth's crust that will be accessible to man would be needed, and, secondly, we would have to know what scientific and technological progress will be made over the period in question.

The real problem, however, is not that of discovering the total quantities that will eventually become available over an unlimited time horizon, but to have some idea of the reserves potentially exploitable under current or foreseeable economic and technological conditions. This will make it possible to estimate whether sufficient time is available for developing the technologies required to meet future conditions, thereby avoiding bottlenecks in the production system.

A calculation of the global reserves of some important metals was carried out; together with fuels, metals are the minerals mentioned most frequently in the context of depletion. The following data and assumptions were used:

(a) at the global level, mining operations currently go down to an average depth of around 300 metres, and in some instances, depths of up to 3000 metres have been reached;

(b) the total reserves revealed to date (i.e., those already exploited and those

---

[1]Barnett, H. J., and Morse, C. *Scarcity and Growth*. Baltimore, Resources for the Future Inc., The Johns Hopkins Press, 1963, 169.

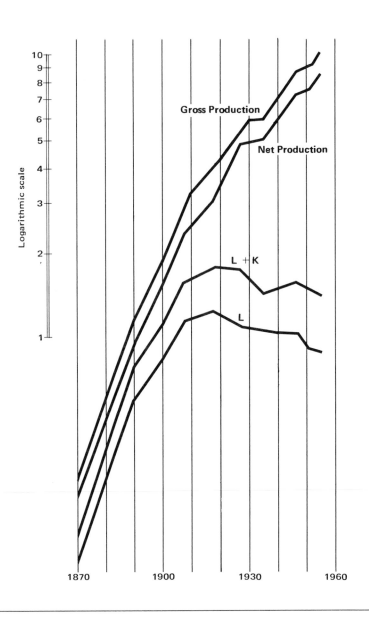

FIGURE 7 (a)

Evolution of mineral production in the USA between 1870 and 1960, giving capital and labour inputs. (From Barnett and Morse 1963.)

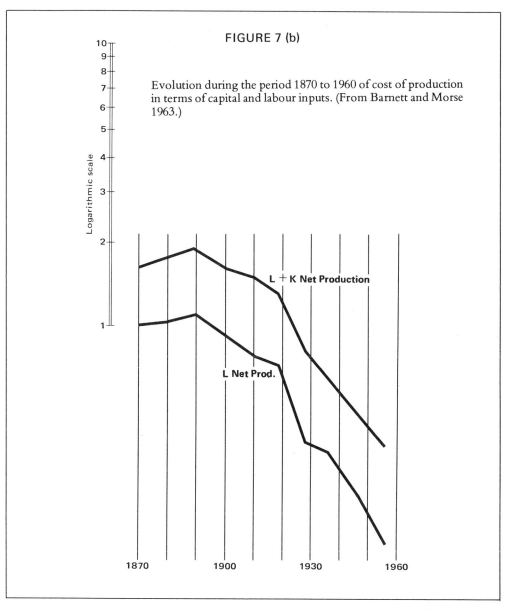

FIGURE 7 (b)

Evolution during the period 1870 to 1960 of cost of production in terms of capital and labour inputs. (From Barnett and Morse 1963.)

L + K Net Production

L Net Prod.

already identified) constitute half the reserves contained in the land component of the crust to an average depth of 300 metres;

(c) the concentration of ore bodies on (or near) the surface remains more or less constant to a depth of around 3000 metres.

Calculations based on these assumptions multiply known reserves severalfold. (Details in: *Natural Resources, Latin American World Model,* Fundación Bariloche, 1975.)

Mineral reserves can increase even without the discovery of new deposits (and, historically, this has been the rule rather than the exception.)

31

Deposits of many metals (particularly copper, manganese, aluminium, titanium, nickel, lead, zinc, and columbium) contain large quantities of low-grade ores that are not normally included in reserve figures. These can be divided into paramarginal (those that can be exploited at a cost one and a half times higher than current costs using current technology), and submarginal (those that could be exploited at costs two or three times higher than at present). This cost gap can be easily overcome by developments in technology, as has been demonstrated time and time again in past decades. What is important, however, is that these reserves increase exponentially with a reduction in the metal concentration. Their exploitation would increase known reserves several times over.

Seabed Resources — In recent years, vast deposits of manganese nodules and sediments on the deep ocean floors have been discovered. These have a large concentration of some of the more important metals (manganese, cobalt, nickel, copper).

Surveys to date have explored only a small area of the ocean floor, but the frequency and density of the nodules discovered so far show that they certainly cover most of the ocean floor. These reserves are sufficient to meet world demand for several centuries at current consumption rates.

At the 1974 Caracas Conference on the control of marine resources, strong evidence was provided of the importance of these deposits. There are companies with definite plans for their exploitation, which are likely to be put into effect in the near future.

The Outlook in the Long Term — This brief analysis indicates that mineral reserves *exploitable with current technology, or that of the near future,* are probably sufficient for many centuries to come.

The Concept of Depletion of Mineral Resources — It is therefore worth thinking about the well-known concept that assumes that because the earth is finite so are its resources. This is obviously true, but the fallacy introduced as irrefutable proof of a final catastrophe is that of confusing finite and *exhaustible*. With very few exceptions, the huge volume of mineral resources in the crust are not lost once they have been mined and used, but continue to form an integral part of the planet's resources. They may be temporarily incorporated into capital or consumption goods; they may be chemically combined with other elements; but despite this, they remain indestructible. Technology has shown its ability to find ways of extracting resources from the most diverse geological formations. It can also recover materials that have already been used once or several times.

Energy

Most of the energy consumed by man is generated from either fossil or nuclear fuels. The availability and cost of energy in the future will thus depend to a great extent on the existence of sufficient deposits of these mineral fuels.

Energy Resources — For the purposes of the model, a study was carried out of the known reserves of the fossil fuels oil, gas, and coal. The conclusion was that hydrocarbons in the form of liquids and gases would probably last about

100 years. For coal it was estimated that, at current consumption rates, there would be enough for about four centuries.

However, the most important fuels for the future are nuclear fuels. Known reserves of uranium in 1970 were 760 000 tonnes of oxide (U_3O_8) costing under $10 per pound (OECD, 1970); production for that year reached 23 000 tonnes.

In this case, as in many others, known reserves form only a small proportion of the total potential reserves. The main reasons for this are: a) uranium has only been sought intensively since the World War II. There remain vast areas to be explored in detail, and deposits below the surface have barely been touched; b) currently, reserves are only exploited if the cost is below $10 per pound. For uranium, the law of exponential growth of reserves with lower ore grade (in this case expressed in value per pound) holds. As a result, a small increase in the price or an advance in technology can greatly increase known exploitable reserves.

Moreover, uranium is one of the elements that is relatively plentiful in the earth's crust; for example, there is more uranium than there is lead. The problem is that it is very scattered. In acid rocks (granite and other rocks derived from it) uranium is found in a concentration of 0.3%, but this is enough for it to constitute a potential reserve that would last almost indefinitely. In seawater it is found in a concentration of 0.3 milligrams per cubic metre.

Studies recently carried out in Sweden show that uranium can be extracted from granite at a cost of just under double the current world price. The U.K. Atomic Energy Commission has reached the conclusion that uranium can be extracted from the sea at a similar cost.[2]

Thus potential reserves of uranium and thorium are sufficient to satisfy the energy requirements for a practically indefinite period. If the problem of producing energy is solved with nuclear fusion, which according to some specialists might occur in the next 20–50 years, energy reserves could possibly surpass the period of biological stability of the human species: they would last for hundreds of millions of years.[3]

The life of different types of fossil fuels will depend to a great extent on the means chosen for producing energy. It is estimated that, by the year 2000, more than half the electricity generated will be provided by nuclear power, and the importance of oil and coal will be reduced. These are more rationally used as petrochemical inputs, rather than as fuels, and the tendency to use them in this way is likely to increase in the future.

In the mathematical model, it is assumed that *costs* of production will remain reasonably constant — that is, with future variations in price being of a similar order to those in the past — for the next 70–80 years. This implies that the cost of production of raw materials, particularly minerals, and of energy will not suffer radical changes.

The Energy Crisis — In the previous section an attempt was made to show

---

[2]Gabor, D. *Innovaciones cinetíficas, technológicas y sociales.* Santiago, Chile, Editorial Universitaria, 1973.

[3]Guillemin, C. *L'avenir de geosciences et le problem de la croissance.* Geologues, No. 24, 1972.

that, from the point of view of physical availability, there is no reason to anticipate problems in the foreseeable future in regard to energy sources.

The increase in the price of oil in recent years has, however, provoked doubts in many sectors about the future stability of world production costs for energy. For this reason, a detailed study was carried out of the so-called energy crisis and its probable future development.[4] The main conclusion of the study is that the energy crisis, which first occurred in the USA, and which since 1967-69 has had an effect internationally, is of a conjunctural character, such as others of similar importance that occurred in the past. And it may already be perceived that the main reactions of the system will be to establish a new equilibrium, which, generally speaking, in the long term will not differ from the previously observed trends.

Pollution

As well as the eventual exhaustion of mineral resources, the growing problem of environmental pollution is often considered to be one of the main obstacles to the achievement of adequate standards of living for mankind. Hence an assessment of its significance is necessary.

As is well known, many discussions of pollution are based on the fact that it is a serious problem in some places, particularly in the industrial centres of rich countries. It would not, however, be valid to generalize from these situations to the world scale, and to predict an imminent collapse of the biosphere. On the other hand, it is true that continuously increasing levels of pollution might eventually produce a general collapse of the various ecosystems of the world.

The most important problem to be considered is whether pollution is a necessary and inevitable consequence of industrial and technological development. Many people, arguing on the basis that technologies that were less damaging to the environment have been replaced since the war by more damaging ones, conclude that *any* industrial development is noxious to the environment.

However, this may not necessarily be the case. For instance, Commoner[5] suggests a period of technological transformation in the U.S. economy, during which there would be a reversal in the trend toward technologies that are damaging to the environment.

Ridker's study[6] of the American situation provides a good illustration of the fact that economic growth is not necessarily accompanied by increased pollution. This study indicates that an active policy of control would lead to pollution levels considerably lower than those existing at present. The cost of pollution control for the USA would be about 2.5% of the GNP for 1980, but, in the year 2000, it would not exceed 2%. Bearing in mind that the level of overall pollution in underdeveloped countries is still very low, it is possible to suppose that control would cost relatively less. This is also the

[4]Suárez, C. *The long-term evolution of the prices of energy.* Buenos Aires, Latin American World Model, Fundación Bariloche, 1974.

[5]Commoner, B. *Ecology and technology resources.* Resources for the Future Inc., 42, 1972, 3–5.

[6]Ridker, R. G. *The economy, resources requirements and pollution level.* In Idker, R. G., ed., Commission on Population Growth and the American Future, Research Reports, Vol. III, Population, Resources and the Environment, 1972.

general conclusion of a study by Syrota.[7]

The problem of local pollution varies quite a lot, depending on whether the country in question is poor or rich. In rich countries, pollution is associated with industrial activity, increasing numbers of vehicles, etc. — in other words, with factors linked to high consumption rates. The control of this type of pollution is possible, given an appropriate abatement policy.

On the other hand, pollution in underdeveloped countries is not so much generated by industrial activity (which is obviously at a much lower level than in the developed countries) but, in general, stems from poverty: polluted water, deficient hygiene attributable to precarious housing conditions and a lack of sewerage, etc. This type of pollution will disappear as basic needs are satisfied, as required in the model.

In conclusion, economic growth is not necessarily associated with an increase in pollution, and, given an active control policy, it can even be reduced at a reasonable cost. At the moment, practically all forms of pollution (with the exception of thermal pollution, which is considered below) are controllable. Therefore, whether to control pollution or not is a political and economic decision. The possibility of controlling it will be increased in the future, as the intensive research currently taking place in this field leads to reduced costs of abatement.

Thermal Pollution — Thermal pollution has special characteristics that differentiate it from other forms of pollution. Its control does not depend to any significant extent on corrective measures (including the increased efficiency of the thermal cycle used) since, for thermodynamic reasons, all the energy generated finally becomes heat.

The effect of thermal pollution on the global biosphere is very difficult to measure precisely. One estimate,[8] based on a world population of 10 000 million and a per capita energy consumption double that of the U.S. in 1970, suggests that the change in the average temperature of the atmosphere would be small (of the order of 0.3 C°) and within the natural variations found in the northern hemisphere.

Estimates of this kind are obviously still very imperfect, and ongoing research could modify them substantially. However, even if thermal pollution will not have a noxious impact on the world in the foreseeable future, it is very probable that it might have some local effects. This is particularly likely in very industrialized areas or those with a high population density. These effects could cause local climatic disturbances that might adversely affect agriculture and other activities.

The most appropriate solution for global pollution — apart from reducing energy consumption to a minimum — is the use of nonpolluting forms of energy: solar, wind, tidal, etc. However, this solution is not realistic in the short or medium term; growth rates in energy consumption are too high, and these nonconventional sources still require considerable technological development before they can be widely used.

There is a new factor related to the thermal problem but still very

---

[7]Syrota, J. *La pollution atmospherique.* Annales des Mines, No. V–VI, 1972, 1–176.

[8]Ponce, V. H. *La contaminación térmica a nivel mundial.* Argentina, Fundación Bariloche, 1973.

35

difficult to evaluate; it is the hypothesis that the average temperature of the atmosphere is dropping. Studies by the Massachusetts Institute of Technology show that, in the period 1958–69, the average temperature of the atmosphere in the northern hemisphere went down by 0.60 C°. The narrowing of the climatic belts that run parallel to the equator (which has resulted in drought in vast regions of Africa), the increased area covered by snow, the increase in the size of ice fields, disturbances in the pattern of monsoons in recent years, and so on, all tend to indicate that the atmosphere is cooling down.

According to some authors, this represents the beginning of a new Ice Age. Others believe that it represents only part of a long-term cyclic oscillation, and will only last a few years. Only careful study will permit evaluation of the true importance of this phenomenon in the future. In any case, this cooling shows that the effect of thermal pollution caused by men has so far been more than compensated for by natural processes.

Conclusions

Natural Resources and Energy — For the reasons set out above, it is assumed in the model that the *production cost* of raw materials and energy will remain essentially constant during the time horizon of the model (1960–2060), that is, apart from any random variations like those observed in the past.

It is also worth pointing out that fuel and nonfuel minerals account for a relatively small proportion of the GNP (2 or 3% between them). This means that a cost increase of, say, 50%, would not significantly affect the long-term development prospects for most countries, but would greatly expand the exploitable resource base (even with current technology).

Pollution — The model assumes that pollution can be controlled and maintained at acceptable levels, if political, social, and economic measures are taken to control it.

Natural resources and pollution do not enter the model as *explicit* variables. They are considered as part of the production costs of various sectors.

Although, as we have attempted to prove, there are no scientific reasons to suppose that either an ecological catastrophe or an acute scarcity of natural resources will occur in the foreseeable future, there is no justification for ignoring these problems. The assumption that there is no appreciable danger in the time horizon envisaged is reasonable; it is based on the fact that technology has, until now, grown at a faster rate than consumption. These assumptions, in referring to natural factors, which are not well understood, inevitably involve a certain, though minimal, degree of risk.

The position taken with respect to the model is that the preservation of natural resources and the environment depends on the type of society envisaged; this will set out the specific measures for control. The model tries to describe a society that is, in principle, compatible with its environment.

The compatibility depends, firstly, on the existence of an economic system that produces those basic and cultural goods that human beings really need, and that thus avoids the destructive use of resources. Even when economic growth increases cultural options, it does so at a sufficiently slow rate to allow development of new resources, as these become necessary, and to permit the noxious effects of pollution to be recognized and countered before serious effects result.

The model assumes that, once basic needs have been satisfied, the growth rate of the economy slows down so that, although the range of social options is still on the increase, the resulting damage to the environment is kept at a low level. This reduction in economic activity implies an increase in leisure time, which in itself represents an increase in the number of cultural options while creating minimal demands on the production sector.

Secondly, the success with which a society adapts to its environment, and to available resources, depends to a great extent on the type of technology used in production. In the developed countries, moderate economic growth would make it possible to gradually reverse the counterecological trend of the productive system that has prevailed up to now.

For the countries of the Third World, the problem consists in finding new paths of development that avoid the dangers currently facing the developed nations. The concept of ecodevelopment, which is being increasingly accepted, could provide a general frame of reference.

Chapter 4

The Mathematical Model

In the previous chapter, it was shown that absolute physical limits to development do not exist, at least for the foreseeable future. This, however, is not sufficient to prove that the specific type of society that we are proposing is also possible; its material viability with current economic resources must be demonstrated.

To test this viability, a mathematical model was built. This chapter outlines its characteristics and properties.

Bearing in mind that the main objective is to establish how and over what time period basic needs can be satisfied, the model essentially represents an economic system, or, more exactly, a production system.

Economic Sectors

The most important economic sectors included in the model are, obviously, those that correspond to basic needs. The sectors included are: (1) nutrition; (2) housing; (3) education; (4) other services and consumer goods; and (5) capital goods.

Sectors 1, 2, and 3 produce the goods necessary for the satisfaction of basic needs. Sector 5 provides the basis for future consumption, and sector 4 refers to all remaining economic activities. The sectors are vertically integrated, and are defined in such a way that intermediate transactions are eliminated.

Three of the five sectors that produce goods can be precisely specified: nutrition, with calories and protein; housing, by number of dwellings; and education, in terms of places available at the basic educational level (first 12 years of formal education).

"Other services and consumer goods" and "capital goods" cannot be measured in this way because they cover a great variety of products. Items such as clothing, furniture, household utensils, health care, transportation, communications, leisure activities, public and administrative services, and all educational activities not in sector 3, are included in sector 4, whereas sector 5 includes construction of housing and planning of the infrastructure of the cities, public buildings, the infrastructure of transportation, communications and other basic services, machinery and vehicles, etc.

The Production Function

For each production sector, the output levels are determined by the inputs of capital and labour, modified by their respective productivities. A Cobb–Douglas function was chosen because it allows substitution between capital and labour to be represented. This characteristic is very important, particularly for the underdeveloped countries, where it is essential to be able

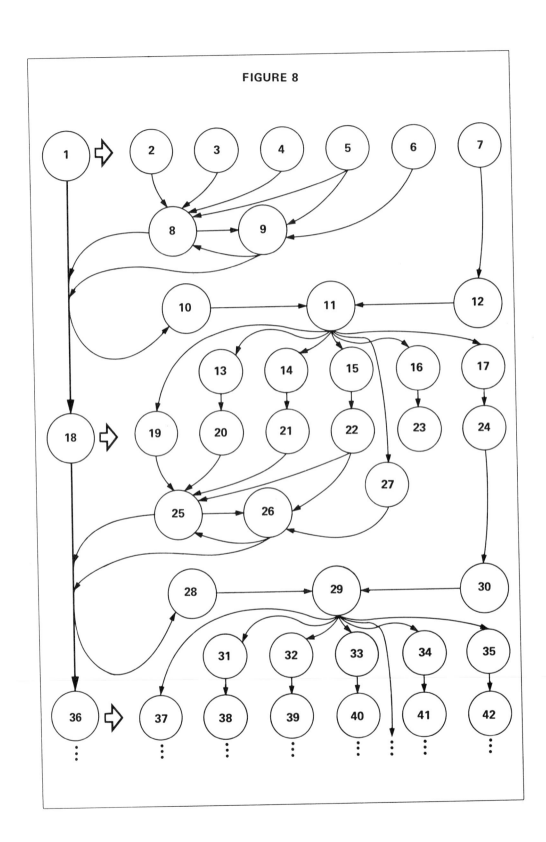

FIGURE 8

to substitute capital with labour.

The economically active population is derived from the demographic model. Data used to initialize the model, including employed population, availability of capital, depreciation, GNP, etc., were obtained from different sources (including, in particular, UN agencies).

Figure 8 is a simplified flowchart of the model. The various subsectors are shown in more detail in later chapters.

Labour Force

In the model, the labour force varies between 1960 and 1980 in accordance with data and projections from the ILO. From then on it is taken as being the same proportion of total population as it was in 1980.

Technological Progress

For the same input of capital and labour, output grows over time; this phenomenon has been observed since the beginning of the Industrial Revolution, but only in the last decades has it been measured with some precision. The increase in productivity is attributed mainly to technological progress, although many experts believe that such factors as improved education and living conditions of the labour force have also influenced it.

The model was initialized using 1960 data, and Table 1 gives the resulting rates of technological progress for the historic period 1960–1970, broken down by sector and region. As can be seen, the rate of technological progress in some key sectors of the economy is greater in underdeveloped regions than in the developed countries. This result, surprising though it may seem at first sight, is easily explained. The developed countries use the most advanced technology available, and therefore an increase in productivity depends mainly on the *creation* of new technology by scientific and

---

Fig. 8. Flowchart of the mathematical model.

1 Total population	22 Initial school enrollment rate
2 Active population secondary sector	23 Quality of consumer goods & services
3 Protein & calories per person	24 Total capital 1982
4 Urbanization rate & houses per family	25 Birthrate
5 Initial school enrollment rate	26 Life expectancy
6 Active population primary sector	27 Active population primary sector
7 Total capital 1980	28 Total labour 1982
8 Birthrate	29 Optimization
9 Life expectancy	30 Total capital 1982
10 Total labour 1981	31 Production protein & calories
11 Optimization	32 Urbanization & housing
12 Total capital 1981	33 Macroeducation: educational places
13 Production of protein & calories	34 Consumer goods & services
14 Urbanization & housing	35 Capital goods
15 Macroeducation: educational places	36 Total population 1982
16 Consumer goods & services	37 Active population secondary sector
17 Capital goods	38 Protein & calories per person
18 Total population 1981	39 Urbanization rate & houses per family
19 Active population secondary sector	40 Initial school enrollment
20 Protein & calories per person	41 Quality of consumer goods & services
21 Urbanization rate & houses per family	42 Total capital 1983

Table 1. Rates of technological progress for the period 1960–70 calculated with the model.

	Food	Housing	Education	Consumer goods	Capital goods
Developed countries	1.32	0.5	0.5	2	2
Latin America	0.5	0.5	1.99	2	2
Africa	0.91	0.5	1.31	3.25	3.48
Asia and Oceania	0.84	0.5	1.89	3.2	3.37

technological research. In the underdeveloped countries, productivity increases rapidly (particularly in sectors producing consumer and capital goods) because of the incorporation of technology that is already available to replace older, less efficient methods of production.

The approach adopted in the model is to utilize coefficients of technological progress that are lower than those observed historically, and to keep them constant for the whole period covered by the runs. This is a conservative but reasonable hypothesis: to project the high rates observed in some countries and regions in recent decades over nearly a century would have been more debatable.

The coefficients for technological progress adopted, by sectors, are the following:

Capital goods	1.5% per annum
Food	1.0% per annum
Housing	1.0% per annum
Education	0.5% per annum
Other goods and services	1.0% per annum

To give some idea of what these rates of technological progress mean, it is worth pointing out that rates of 1% and 1.5% per annum lead to a doubling of productivity in 70 and 47 years, respectively.

The Division of the World into Regions

One of the most important problems to be resolved when building a world model is the degree of geographic aggregation to be applied. The choice between different alternatives clearly depends on the purpose of the model and on the information available.

This model is designed to show over what time periods and under what conditions (starting with current economic resources) it would be possible to achieve the proper satisfaction of the basic needs. As the initial situation — i.e., the economic resources available and degree to which needs are currently satisfied — is very different for different countries, it was necessary to group them into regions whose socioeconomic indicators are relatively homogeneous. Regional collaboration was also taken into account, particularly for underdeveloped countries, and forms one of the key elements in the attainment of the proposed society. This depends, to a great extent, on geographical proximity.

From these considerations, the following regions were established: the first (Region 1) contains all the developed countries. The other three regions

Table 2. Main socioeconomic indicators for each of the regions in 1960.

	Developed countries	Latin America	Africa	Asia
Population (*millions*)	946	208	257	1544
Calories/capita/day	2980	2440	2268	1985
Protein/capita/day	98.7	60.3	51.2	51.1
Enrollment[a]	84.8	48	24.3	41.3
GNP	1401	372	137	90
Life expectancy at birth	69.2	55.8	43.3	48
Natality (*children born/ 1000 inhabitants*)	21.3	40.4	46.5	37.8
Houses/family	0.71	0.50	0.43	0.44

[a]Enrollment: percentage of people between 7 and 18 years of age in the education system. Calculated from the total number of people between these ages.

are: Latin America and the Caribbean (Region 2); Africa (Region 3); and Asia and Australasia, plus Turkey, but excluding the USSR (Region 4). Differences between socialist and capitalist countries are not made explicit in the mathematical model.[9]

Table 2 gives the value of the main socioeconomic indicators for each of the regions in 1960.

International Trade

International trade is included in the model in the form of the aggregate value of imports and exports of regions, disaggregated by sectors. The sectors affected are capital goods, other goods and services, and food. Each region is almost self-sufficient in education and housing, the very small external inputs required being included in capital and consumer goods. The initial values used are those for 1970.

Table 3 gives the aggregated results of those exchanges, in terms of balance of payments and the percentage of GNP that these figures represent for each region.

The fundamental assumptions used for international trade in the model are as follows:

(*a*) As the data for 1960 are not complete, it is assumed that the global level of trade of each block for that year is proportional to its total GNP, taking 1970 as the base year. The volume of trade for each sector in 1960, as well as for the years after 1970, is assumed to be proportional to its contribution to the total GNP, taking also 1970 as the base year.

(*b*) The disequilibrium in the balance of payments of the regions is gradually reduced, until equilibrium is reached in 20 years from the time of implementation of the policies proposed (1980).

The equilibrium hypothesis is reasonable in the context of the economic policy proposed. In any case, the balance of payment does not affect the total production capacity of each region, since, to import a certain quantity of goods it is necessary to produce other goods of equivalent value for

---

[9]Capitalist and socialist countries are not differentiated because all countries are supposed to follow the same policy after 1980 (see page 13).

exchange. In the model, each region is taken as an economic unit, which presupposes total collaboration between the countries forming it. The satisfaction of the basic needs — food, housing, education and health — is achieved in all regions with the use of almost exclusively local economic resources. The reduction in consumption in less essential sectors, together with regional collaboration, will also contribute to the reduction of dependence on imported goods.

Operation of the Model

Mathematical models built to describe the evolution in time of a set of variables (in this case, population and other demographic variables, food intake per capita per day, housing per family, etc.) must include interrelations that make it possible to calculate values for a particular year using the values of the previous year. Starting from a given situation, the model runs through a number of years, and gives the values of the various indicators at the end of the period.

Initial data on the economically active population, together with availability and productivity of capital, determine for each period the levels of production in the five sectors of the model. For the initial year (1960), real-world data are used; values for the years after that are generated by the model.

The base year 1960 was used because, first, it is the earliest year for which there is relatively complete information about the principal variables used; and secondly, the behaviour of the model during the first few years of its operation can be compared with real-world data.

Each sectorial product is expressed using a production function of the Cobb–Douglas type, thus:

$$\text{product} = (\text{capital allocated})^\alpha \times (\text{wages paid to labour})^{1-\alpha}$$

α is a power that expresses the relative weights of capital and labour in the product; its value lies between 0 and 1.

The model uses a system of costs that is derived as follows. Taking food as an example, the gross product in this sector (in money terms) is known. From the consumption per capita and the total population, the total number of calories produced in 1960 can be calculated. The cost of a calorie is then:

$$\text{cost} = \frac{\text{total value produced}}{\text{total calories produced}}.$$

Table 3. Balance-of-payments by region (1970).[a]

Region	Balance-of-payments in millions of dollars (1970)	% of 1970 GNP
Developed countries	13.215	0.635
Latin America	−3.757	3.15
Asia	−5.347	2.42
Africa	−4.618	9.05

[a]Excluding the People's Republic of China and the USSR.

44

For housing and education, the costs are calculated in a similar way. As will be seen later, these costs make it possible to calculate, for the succeeding years, the physical production of sectors catering for basic needs. The need, or demand, for the goods and services provided by these sectors is determined by the size (and other characteristics) of the population in each year, which makes it possible to establish, first, food requirements; secondly, the need for housing, from the average size of a family; and thirdly, from the age structure of the population, the number of persons requiring basic education (all persons between 6 and 17 years of age) and the size of the potential labour force (all persons between 18 and 64). All this information is provided by the population submodel, whose main features are described in the next chapter.

Once the potential labour force is known, the other piece of information required for the production function is capital, for which data are available for the initial year (1960). Total capital for a given year is equal to capital in the previous year, plus that part of the gross product generated by sector 5 (capital goods) in the previous year, less depreciation.

Running the Model

We shall start by briefly explaining the behaviour of the model for the historical period for which real-world data are available. This provides a check of the accuracy with which the model reproduces real-world behaviour.

Having obtained the total capital and labour force for the year following the base year, it is necessary to distribute them between the different sectors. Then, using the production function, it is possible to calculate the product generated by each sector; added together, these give the new total product.

As there is little data on this distribution after 1960, it was assumed that it remained constant from then onward. The possible error introduced by this assumption is compensated for, as we will see later, by an adjustment of the model.

Once the new sectoral products are known, physical production is obtained from their costs. For example, given the new gross product of the food sector, we have:

$$\text{total calories produced} = \frac{\text{total value of production}}{\text{unit cost}}.$$

As the new total population is known from the population submodel, per capita consumption of calories and protein can easily be calculated. Similarly, by using costs, it is possible to calculate the number of houses and the educational enrollment for the year.

From these values, the demographic sector derives the new population, and the cycle begins again.

Calibration of the Model

Through the general process outlined above, the model is run forward to 1970, the last year for which complete information exists for all the indicators employed. Given that the parameters of the production function are known within some margin of error, together with the distribution of the gross product by sectors, it is possible to make adjustments — still within the

45

Table 4. Results of the model for 1970.

	Developed countries		Latin America		Africa		Asia	
	RV[a]	CV[a]	RV	CV	RV	CV	RV	CV
Life expectancy (years)	70.1	70.4	61.8	61.0	45.9	46.2	50.2	50.2
Gross product/capita (U.S. $)	2029	2023	445	440	169	154	113	112
Enrollment in education (%)	97.5	96.6	60	58.8	28.4	27.8	[b]	39.8
Calories/capita/day	3063	2992	2472	2423	2254	2322	2054	2080
Birthrate (/1000)	17.3	16.6	38	34.7	45.9	44.1	38.3	40.7
Crude mortality (/1000)	9.2	10.6	9.1	9.0	20.3	18.7	15.4	16.4
Population size (millions)	1056	1032	277	271	330	335	1940	1965

Predictions of life expectancy in 1960

	Developed countries	Latin America	Africa	Asia
Real values	69.2	55.8	43.3	48.6
Model values	69.3	55.6	43.5	48.3

[a]RV, real value; CV, calculated value.
[b]No data available for the People's Republic of China.

margin of error allowed — so that the main indicators supplied by the model for 1970 are as close as possible to the known values for that year. To establish the closest fit for the parameters a special optimization process was used.

Table 4 compares the results of the model with real values for 1970. As can be seen, the differences are small and show the high degree of accuracy obtained.

The Proposed Social Policy, and the Process of Optimization

The model can be run forward to any year after 1970. In the runs presented here, it is assumed that the social policy outlined in Chapter 2 will be implemented from 1980 (the "base" year). The selection of that year is of course arbitrary and was chosen because it was considered to be a reasonable time after the publication of these results. The "base" year can be varied simply by altering the period for which the model runs forward before the proposed policies are implemented. The procedure adopted to verify the feasibility of the proposed socioeconomic policy is set out below.

Socioeconomic planning can be characterized in our context as a problem of optimal allocation of capital and labour provided that the targets are known.

One target could be to maximize GNP, starting from the assumption that the faster the rate of economic growth, the sooner it is possible to attain the desired level of well–being. Another could be to maximize output of the basic needs, and another, to maximize life expectancy at birth.

46

After analysis of these and other possibilities, it was decided to opt for maximization of *life expectancy at birth* (LE). The model therefore allocates capital and labour in such a way as to maximize life expectancy at each moment in the run. The reasons that led to the choice of this indicator are set out in the next section.

Apart from trying to maximize life expectancy at birth, the model also has to meet certain other constraints or conditions. Some of these are the result of the theoretical formulation of the economic model, and others stem from socioeconomic considerations. The main socioeconomic limitation consists in ensuring that the level of satisfaction of any one of the basic needs cannot, in any year, be lower than it was in the previous year. Several other controls, introduced in the form of constraints, make it possible for the model to adapt to changing situations, indicating for each case the strategy to be followed. When a conflict arises between meeting different objectives, the optimizing mechanism sacrifices one or more of them, according to a predetermined order of priorities. The computation of the optimal strategy is carried out by means of a special nonlinear optimization algorithm.

Although the model was designed to satisfy the basic features of the outline for a proposed society, its structure makes it possible to work with different hypotheses. For example, it would be possible to evaluate the effects of collaboration between different regions; to modify productivity in any sector so as to study the effects of different rates of technological progress; to use other production functions; to vary working hours or the manpower available for any one sector; or to optimize with respect to other variables; and so on.

Chapter 5

Demography and Health

Population

The Population Submodel — The population submodel attempts to identify the specific factors in economic and social development that influence the demographic evolution of society.

In almost all models built to date, population has been entered as an exogenous factor. Demographic projections carried out by the United Nations, or other international or national organizations, have been used to provide forecasts of population size. Models built on this basis do not incorporate the interrelation between demographic and socioeconomic variables.

This procedure was not applicable to this world model, since one of its objectives is to establish the extent to which changes in socioeconomic factors affect population growth and other demographic indicators, such as life expectancy at birth, infant and crude death rates, etc. In other words, an attempt is made to explain demographic evolution as a function of socioeconomic variables.

Therefore, to build the population submodel, variables that are most critical in determining population were taken for all countries and a system was designed that made it possible to study the functional relationships between them. This was done by using multivariable, linear, and nonlinear analyses to build accurate regression models.

The results are synthesized in Fig. 9, which shows the variables used and the relationships between them. The plus or minus sign that appears on the lines connecting variables indicates whether the relationship is positive or negative, that is, whether an increase in one produces an immediate increase or reduction in the other.

Finally, a model built by CELADE (Centro Latinoamericano de Demografía), which requires as inputs the structure of the population by age and sex, life expectancy at birth, and total fecundity of year t, was adapted to calculate the new population of the year $t + 1$.

In this model, as can be seen in Fig. 9, the main demographic variables — life expectancy at birth (and, as a result, total and child mortalities), birthrates, and average family size — are expressed as functions of seven socioeconomic variables: population employed in the secondary sector; school enrollment (see education); houses per family; caloric and protein intake per capita per day; population employed in agriculture; and a measure of urbanization. Knowing natality, total fecundity can be calculated, and combining this with the age structure of the population the fertility of women between 15 and 49 can be obtained. From all these elements, the model calculates population year by year and its structure by age and sex.

FIGURE 9

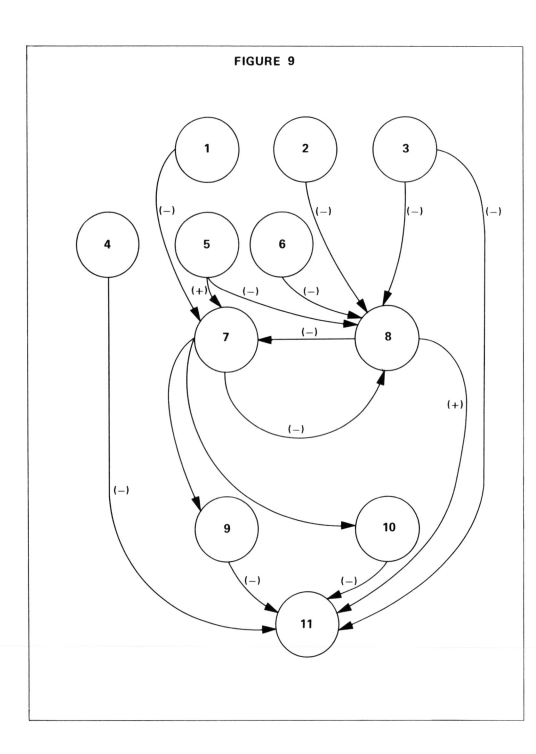

50

The correlations obtained between real-world data and calculated values are as follows:

Life expectancy at birth	+0.95
Birthrate	+0.90
Persons in each family	+0.75

In interpreting calculated life expectancy values, the active population in agriculture is an important influence on overall life expectancy as is confirmed by historical data. This is because, in most countries, the rural population has little or no access to services such as education, health, etc.

However, in the model it is assumed that the rural population will be gradually grouped in communities of a size that makes it possible to provide the essential services. Consequently, in the long term, the effect of the population employed in agriculture on life expectancy will decrease as the rural population gradually acquires urban living standards (see Chapter 6).

In the model, using a function that incorporated the negative effect on average life expectancy from the rural sector throughout the period considered, the highest life expectancy achieved was 71.5 years. In runs where the population employed in agriculture was not included, a life expectancy of 75.6 years was achieved. This last figure is probably more realistic, since it coincides approximately with what is considered to be the present average biological limit.

In summary, the model indicates the time scale in which improvement in socioeconomic conditions is likely to make the maximum life expectancy possible. Its absolute biological value is possibly a little higher than the figure given by the model.

Obviously, the model does not assume that the variables used to predict demographic evolution are the only important factors. There are cultural and religious values, amongst other things, that are significant but difficult to quantify. Nonetheless, the results are very satisfactory from the point of view of the precision achieved, and make it possible to predict population changes resulting from the socioeconomic variables considered in the model.

Care must be taken not to confuse functional relationships with causal relationships. This is an empirical model that shows that there is a high correlation between demographic variables and certain socioeconomic variables, but in no way does it attempt to define the mechanisms that cause these links.

Demography and Economic Growth — As can be seen in the model, concrete factors such as food, housing, and education affect the demographic variables. Therefore, for economic growth to have an effect on population, it should have as its objective the satisfaction of the basic needs of the majority of the community. In most of the underdeveloped countries economic growth does not fulfill this condition; for this reason in these countries there

---

Fig. 9. Variables used to build the population submodel, and relationships between them.

1 Active population in agriculture	7 Life expectancy at birth
2 Active population in secondary sector	8 Birthrate
3 Houses per family	9 Infant mortality
4 Urbanization	10 Crude death rate
5 School enrollment	11 Persons per family
6 Calories	

is no significant correlation between population growth and economic growth as expressed in terms of GNP.

This argument is reinforced by the experience of a group of countries that in recent years has carried out active family planning programmes. In some of them — People's Republic of China, South Korea, Malaysia, Republic of China (Taiwan), Chile, Costa Rica, Cuba, and Egypt — there has been a perceptible reduction in fertility. In others — India, Pakistan, Indonesia, Iran, the Philippines, and Nepal — fertility has not varied, although some of them (particularly India and Pakistan) have carried out the most prolonged and intense campaigns to control population.

All the countries in the first group have considerably improved the general conditions of their populations in recent years, in some cases through internal, sociopolitical change (e.g., People's Republic of China, Cuba, Egypt, and Chile). In others, like South Korea and Taiwan, general conditions have improved because of their special position in the international scene, and because of help received, particularly from the USA. On the other hand, the standard of living of the population in all the countries in the second group has remained more or less constant.

Consequently, although it is difficult to differentiate the effects of family planning campaigns from the effects of improved living conditions in countries where there was a reduction in fertility, it seems clear that improved living standards are at least a prerequisite for the success of family planning. The historical evidence and demographic evolutions of the countries mentioned suggest that an improved condition of well-being is the most important factor in reducing fertility.

One of the main objectives of the model is to show whether it is possible to improve living conditions of the population and attain an adequate degree of development through the optimum use of existing resources, without the imposition of birth control. This is not a rejection of all forms of family planning; it assumes that any policy in this direction can only be decided, either individually or collectively, by societies that have reached adequate levels of education, participation, and access to information. In no way is it acceptable to have birth control imposed compulsorily, either directly or indirectly.

Health

It has not been possible to find a single indicator that provides an adequate measure of health in a country or region. However, much research has been carried out on the subject and it is possible to affirm that, for a first approximation, there are at least two indicators that should be considered: life expectancy at birth, and infant mortality.

These two indicators are strongly dependent on the socioeconomic factors incorporated in the model. Thus the degree of health of the population, as measured through these variables, is affected by changes in socioeconomic conditions resulting from the application of the social policy advocated in the model.

Other variables were tested during the construction of the model, such as the number of doctors and beds per inhabitant, but the attempt had to be abondoned because these indicators proved to be statistically irrelevant. Among the possible reasons for this were:

(a) the lack of standard criteria for calculating medical staff and number of beds;

(*b*) the high correlation of indicators with others, such as urbanization, housing, education, etc., which are already included in the model.

At any rate, the results of the model coincide with empirical observations in confirming that the general sanitary condition of the population depends more on general living conditions than on specific investments in health.

Health expenditure and investment is included in sector 4 of the economic system.

Life Expectancy at Birth and the Optimization Technique

As was pointed out above, three possible optimization criteria were considered: Gross national product (GNP), basic needs, and life expectancy at birth.

GNP is the indicator that has been most used in economic planning and has been severely criticized in recent years. The satisfaction of basic needs appeared to be a criterion for optimization that was much more in tune with the objectives of the model. However, bearing in mind that the nature of these needs is very different, as are the social efforts required to satisfy them, the problem of establishing priorities between them arises.

To solve this, it is necessary to evaluate the effect on the population of different alternatives in the allocation of resources to each one of the basic needs. This is done by the optimization of life expectancy at birth.

The reasons that finally led to this choice are its significance as an indicator of the level of well-being of the population and its advantages from the operational point of view.

Life expectancy at birth is, without doubt, the indicator that best reflects general conditions of life regardless of country. Its value is a function of the extent to which the basic needs are satisfied and of other factors, such as urbanization, that most affect the lives of the members of a community.

Besides, life expectancy measures the degree to which a society allows its members to attain one of their essential rights: to live a life that is as long as is biologically possible. This is an absolute right that no society can ignore. In general, the lives of the members of a society can be regulated to some extent, but this specific right is an inalienable attribute of each human being.

The operational advantages of optimizing life expectancy at birth are clear from Fig. 9. Life expectancy at birth is a variable that is a function of socioeconomic factors and provides a measure of well-being that is used during model runs to allocate resources between sectors.

Once this indicator had been chosen for optimization there were two possible alternative approaches:
(*a*) to attain the maximum possible life expectancy for each year;
(*b*) to attain the desired life expectancy in the minimum time.

To minimize the time required, techniques of mathematical economics and optimization have been developed; unfortunately, these techniques require an excessively long computing time, even with the fastest computers available. Therefore, it was decided to optimize life expectancy year by year, but while introducing a great number of constraints to ensure (among other things) an adequate rate of investment for the satisfaction of future needs and the harmonious evolution of the main socioeconomic variables.

53

Chapter 6

Food

According to FAO estimates, the quantity of food currently produced is sufficient to satisfy the needs of everybody in the world. It is also well known that, for the time being, physical limits do not restrict the production of food; only 43% of potentially arable land is being used, and even using conservative estimates, yields are much lower than those theoretically possible.

If there are no physical limits at present, why is a high proportion of the world's population undernourished? The answer can be summarized as follows. The true causes of hunger have their roots in sociopolitical factors, at both the international and national levels. Especially important in underdeveloped countries are local factors of social and political organization that hinder the equitable distribution and production of food. In most of those developing countries that have capitalist economies, the production of food is based on market demand, and, as most of the population has very little purchasing power, demand is not enough to stimulate production. The division of land also contributes to production deficiencies, because land becomes, to a great extent, the subject of speculation and the symbol of power and social prestige, rather than a factor of production. Other contributing factors are deficiencies in the general infrastructure of transport, storage, distribution, and so on, which mean that a considerable proportion of the food produced in the most needy countries is lost before it reaches the market.

It is evident that, if the sociopolitical factors that hinder production and distribution of food were modified, the problems of hunger and undernourishment could be solved. There remains, however, the question that has become the centre of one of the most important debates of the moment: *Will it be possible to feed everybody in the future?*

The food sector or submodel has been built to help answer this question, and others, such as: Will it be possible to feed humanity adequately in the future? What is the most efficient way of producing food, and at what cost?

The food sector is composed of three subsectors: agriculture; livestock, which includes all animals that can be used as food, except game; and fisheries. A fourth subsector, nonconventional sources of food, which includes the cultivation of algae and bacteria, marine agriculture, direct synthesis of protein, purification of protein from nonnutritious plants, etc., has not been included because, apart from its complexities and heterogeneity, all the information comes from laboratory experiments or theoretical extrapolations. There is very little trustworthy information on the viability of these processes at the world level. In any case, the model indicates that

55

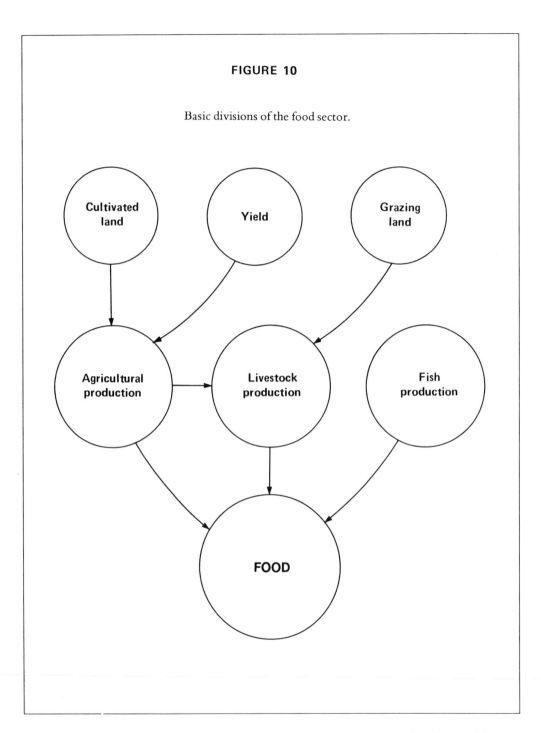

FIGURE 10

Basic divisions of the food sector.

nonconventional food sources would not be necessary in the foreseeable future.

The main subdivisions in the sector are shown in Fig. 10.

Agriculture

The agricultural subsector is the most important one for the production of food, because of its current contribution to total production and because of its potential capacity in the future.

The general outline of the sector is basically simple. Production depends on two factors: the area of land in use, and yields per unit area. Land usable for agriculture is *potential arable land*, only a fraction of which is really used at a given time *(cultivated land)*. If an increase in the arable land area is required, it is necessary to develop new land, and that involves costs. The quantity of arable land can also decrease through *degradation* and *urbanization*.

Yield, which in general terms is expressed as the quantity of agricultural output per unit area, is influenced by the type of soil, although this factor is increasingly less important in modern agriculture; the dominant factors include the climate, and, above all, the technology used (fertilizers, pesticides, mechanization, etc.).

Finally, not all the produce reaches the market. A very considerable proportion, particularly in developing countries, is lost in transportation, storage, and distribution.

The characteristics of the sector are dealt with in some detail below.

The Land

Potential Arable Land — The concept of potential arable land depends on the technology applied and includes all land whose soil is considered suitable for crops adapted to the local conditions.

Estimates used to determine the amount of potential arable land include Africa, Asia, Australasia, Europe, North America, South America, and the Soviet Union. These estimates are given in Table 5, along with figures for land actually under cultivation.

Potential arable land is considered fixed for each region; it could only increase with the advent of new technologies, such as economic desalination of sea water. Cultivated land (land currently being cultivated, temporarily or permanently) can increase if new land is cultivated and degradation can be reduced.

Degradation of the soil can be due to reduced fertility of the soil, soil erosion, or urbanization. In the model it is assumed that:

(a) the cost of preserving the fertility of the soil is 10% of all inputs. In this way, fertility degradation becomes an economic, rather than a physical, factor:

(b) the cost of effective control of erosion is approximately 5% of agricultural inputs:

(c) the rate of urbanization is provided by the Housing and Urbanization Sector (Chapter 7) and it is accepted that society should attempt to reduce building on land that could be used for agriculture. It is considered, as a conservative hypothesis, that in the future only 50% of urbanization will take place on potentially cultivatable land.

The amount of land under cultivation can be increased through the development of new areas until the limit imposed by the availability of

Table 5. Actual and potential arable land.

Region (1970)	Total surface[a]	Potential arable land	Cultivated land	Cultivated land as % of potential arable land	Potential arable land as % of total surface
Developed countries	5498	1093	634	58.0	20
Latin America	2056	736	123	16.7	36
Asia	2753	627	444	70.8	23
Africa	3030	732	204	27.8	24

[a]Includes internal waters.

potentially cultivatable land is reached. Development has a cost and hence depends on the economic resources available.

To determine these costs, an analysis was carried out of a number of estimates made for various development projects in different countries. The projects included the development of areas that had, and had not, been occupied, and of land that had, and had not, been irrigated previously.

The most noticeable feature to emerge from the analysis of the data is the high variability between unit costs in different projects, both between countries and within them.

In the model, a pessimistic hypothesis is taken; it is assumed that the cost per unit increases exponentially with the development of new land, as the remaining fraction of potential arable land is reduced, up to a maximum of $6000 per hectare. The minimum cost per hectare is assumed to be $1200.

Yield — This is defined as the edible output per hectare. Yield depends on many factors: hours of sunshine, temperature, water, carbon dioxide, soil nutrients, species or variety of the plant, etc.

Agricultural yields have increased spectacularly this century, and this trend appears to be continuing. The rate of growth in yield has always been higher in developed countries. Figure 11(*a*) shows the increases in yield obtained for cereals in each region for the period 1950–71.

For the purposes of the model, production of food is measured by weight, by calories, and by protein; statistics published by FAO give figures only by weight. To calculate the caloric and protein content, specific conversion factors were used for each important crop.

The FAO also provides estimates of the area under cultivation by type of crop. The total production by weight of all crops in one region, divided by the total area under cultivation, gives the aggregated yield per hectare.

Figure 11(*b*) gives the actual values for aggregated yield in 1970 by region, expressed in tonnes of edible product.

The study began from the hypothesis that a nation's aggregated yield is directly related to the level of inputs, and, as these are indicators of the level of technology, a study was made of the correlation between yield and various types of agricultural input. The inputs considered were those for which there are statistics for the whole world.

Information on inputs was obtained from FAO sources. The population economically employed in agriculture was also considered as an input.

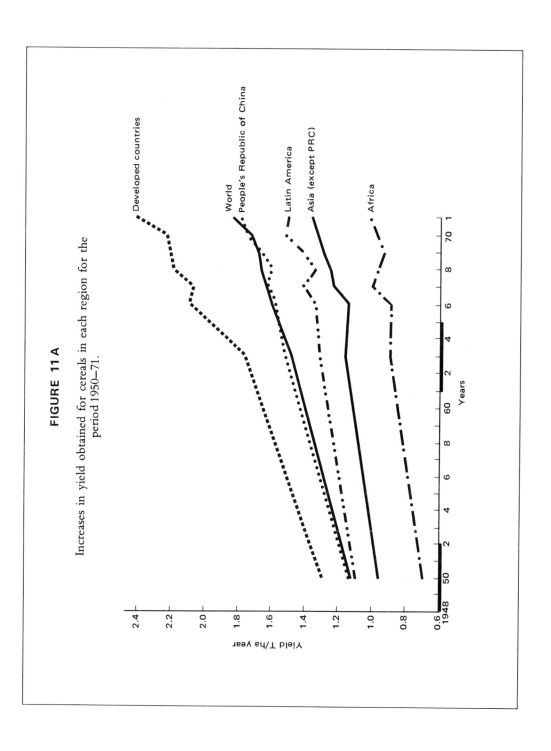

FIGURE 11 A

Increases in yield obtained for cereals in each region for the period 1950–71.

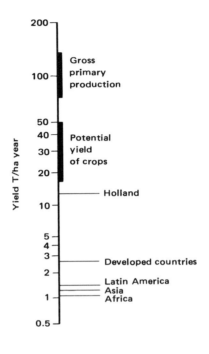

FIGURE 11 B

Actual value of aggregated yield in 1970 by region, expressed in tonnes of edible product.

Fertilizers — The FAO provides data on production and consumption of fertilizers in terms of their content of plant nutrients. The consumption of nitrogen, phosphate, and potash fertilizers was aggregated to give the total consumption of fertilizers for a country.

Pesticides — Available data refer to the quantity of pesticides (insecticides, fungicides, fumigants, herbicides, rodent killers, and other pesticides) used or sold for agricultural use. Pesticides are listed, where possible, in terms of their active ingredients.

Tractors — FAO data include tractors, garden tractors, harvesters, combine harvesters, and milking equipment. In this study, it was decided to take tractors as a global indicator of mechanization because they are the commonest mechanized equipment used and, secondly, because information on other mechanical equipment is very incomplete.

Agricultural Population and Population Economically Active in Agriculture — Agricultural population includes all those persons (and their unemployed

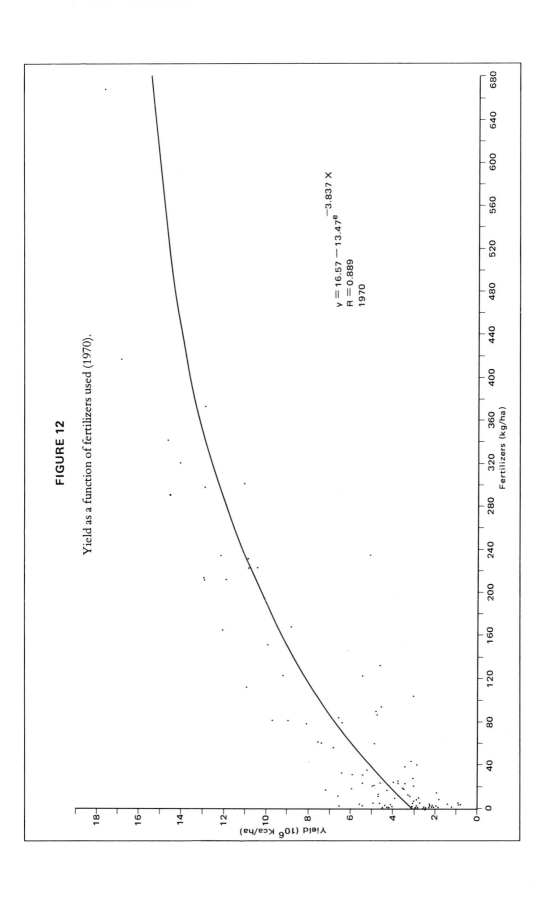

FIGURE 12

Yield as a function of fertilizers used (1970).

$y = 16.57 - 13.47e^{-3.837\,X}$
$R = 0.889$
1970

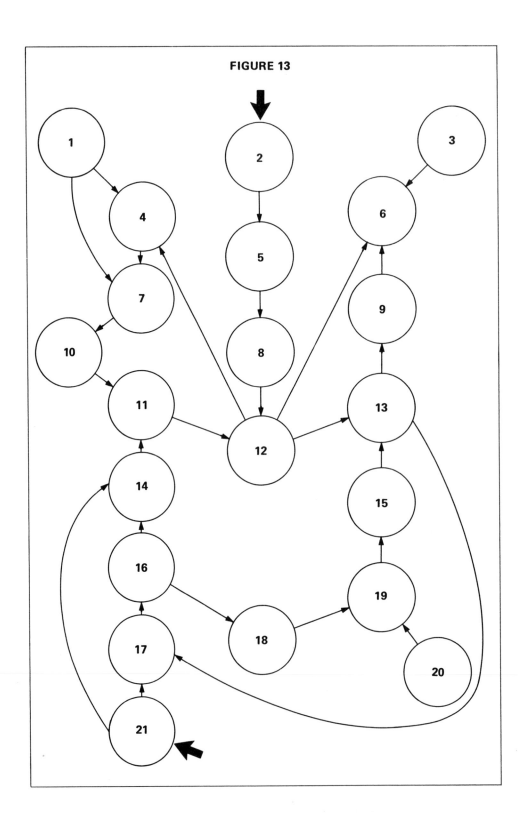

FIGURE 13

dependents) whose incomes depend on agriculture. For the purposes of this definition, agriculture includes forestry, fishing, and hunting. The population economically active in agriculture includes all those people who participate directly in this economic activity, as employees, self-employed workers, salaried staff, or unpaid workers who help in the operation of a family for farm business. Data are for 1965.

The analysis of data does not indicate a significant cross-correlation between different agricultural inputs, with the exception of fertilizers and tractors; other inputs only show weak cross-correlations.

The quantity of fertilizers used can be considered to be a good indicator of the level of efficiency in agriculture. For this reason, fertilizer consumption is the most important variable in this sector.

Several equations were used to fit the data for aggregated yield as a function of fertilizer consumed. The exponential function in Fig. 12 was adopted finally, since this most closely matched the data for 1970.

In the model, the pessimistic hypothesis that the maximum yield obtainable (4 tonnes per hectare) is about half the current maximum average aggregated yield by country is adopted. In using this function, it is implicitly assumed that the relative composition of crops remains fixed at 1970 values; this is also a pessimistic assumption, since one way of increasing yield for a given input level is to increase the relative proportion of high-yielding varieties. As will be seen later, the model does allow yield to depend on inputs other than fertilizers.

Not all arable land is sown each year with basic food products; some must be left fallow, and some must be used for nonfood crops and for various minor food crops. The relationship between land usable for the main food crops, cultivable land, and permanently cultivated land was calculated for the year 1970.

The Cost of Agricultural Inputs — It is assumed that agricultural inputs are used every year in each region. The cost of fertilizers was taken to be $500 per tonne of nutrients as calculated by FAO. This includes the cost of capital required for extracting the fertilizers, for manufacture, and for distribution.

Although fertilizers are a fundamental agricultural input, other inputs must also be used in appropriate proportions to maximize yield. After analyzing available data, it was decided to allocate a fixed proportion (20%) of the capital available for agricultural inputs to all inputs other than fertilizers.

Fig. 13. Flowchart of the agriculture subsector.

1 Potential arable land
2 Total urbanization rate
3 Processing losses
4 Potential arable land not yet under cultivation
5 Urbanization rate of arable land
6 Food production from agriculture
7 Fraction of potential arable land remaining
8 Degradation rate of arable land
9 Yield
10 Unit development cost of land
11 Land development rate
12 Arable land under cultivation
13 Fertilizers per ha
14 Available capital for land development
15 Fertilizers available
16 Capital for agricultural inputs
17 Fertilizers
18 Capital for investment in new fertilizers
19 Additional fertilizers produced per year
20 Unit cost of production of new fertilizers
21 Capital for agriculture

63

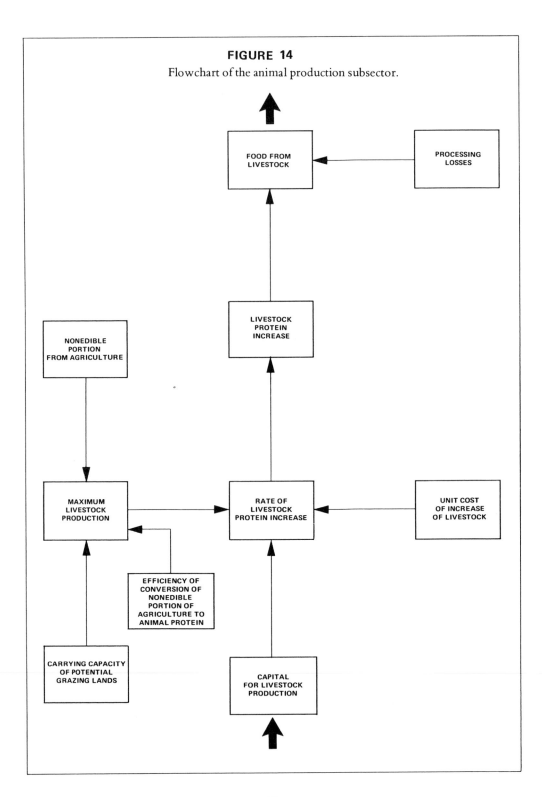

FIGURE 14
Flowchart of the animal production subsector.

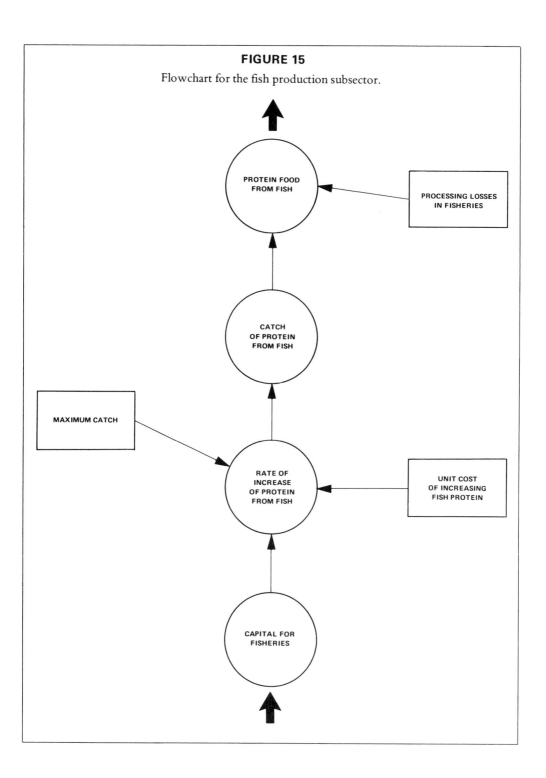

FIGURE 15

Flowchart for the fish production subsector.

PROTEIN FOOD
FROM FISH

PROCESSING LOSSES
IN FISHERIES

CATCH
OF PROTEIN
FROM FISH

MAXIMUM CATCH

RATE OF
INCREASE
OF PROTEIN
FROM FISH

UNIT COST
OF INCREASING
FISH PROTEIN

CAPITAL FOR
FISHERIES

65

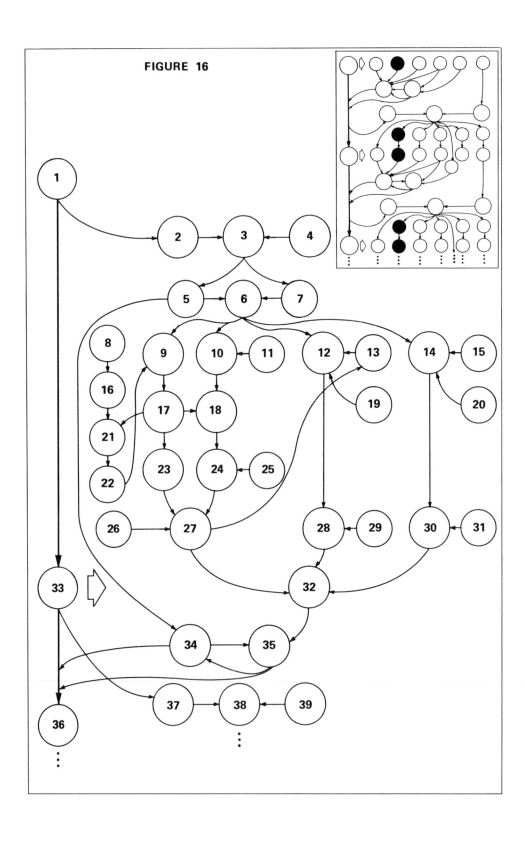

FIGURE 16

In the model, therefore, the economic resources available for agricultural inputs in a given year are distributed in fixed proportions between inputs other than fertilizers, erosion control, and the conservation of soil fertility. The remaining resources are allocated to increased fertilizer production.

Losses after the Harvest — The arable subsector uses the actual yields obtained in each country, rather than the potential yields, and therefore preharvest losses are already accounted for. It is necessary, however, to consider separately losses after the harvest, i.e., those incurred from the moment of harvesting to the time the produce reaches the consumer. The biggest losses are incurred in storage, processing, transportation, and distribution.

On the basis of a considerable number of estimates, it was decided to assume a loss of 10% in developed countries, and 30% in underdeveloped countries. Losses after harvest in underdeveloped countries are gradually reduced (after optimization begins) until they reach 10% in 20 years.

Figure 13 is a flowchart of the agriculture subsector.

Animal Produce

Food of animal origin is important mainly as a source of "high quality protein," i.e., proteins with a high content of essential amino acids that cannot be synthesized by man. However, they can be replaced by those of vegetable origin, if these are improved by the addition of the missing amino acids or protein concentrates. In the model, it is assumed that the latter has been done, and so animal proteins are not differentiated from vegetable proteins.

Because of the strong preference for animal products in many developed and some underdeveloped countries, animals are fed with cereals that could

---

Fig. 16. Structure and operation of the food sector during optimization.

1 Total population 1980	21 Land remaining
2 Total labour force 1980	22 Cost of new land
3 Optimization	23 Cultivated land
4 Total capital 1980	24 Agricultural yield
5 Agricultural labour force	25 Maximum agricultural yield
6 Production function	26 Processing losses
7 Agricultural capital	27 Calories & protein from agriculture
8 Land degradation rate due to urbanization	28 Animal calories & protein
9 New land: rate	29 Processing losses
10 Inputs: rate of increase	30 Fish calories & protein
11 Cost of inputs	31 Processing losses
12 Animal production: increase	32 Calories & protein per capita
13 Maximum animal production	33 Total population 1981
14 Fish catch: increase	34 Life expectancy at birth
15 Maximum fish catch	35 Birthrate
16 Potential arable land	36 Total population 1982
17 Arable land	37 Total labour force 1981
18 Current inputs per ha	38 Optimization
19 Animal production cost	39 Total capital 1981
20 Fish costs	

be used for human consumption. From a global viewpoint, this procedure is irrational, since the efficiency of conversion of forage by animals into animal protein is very low (15% on average). To produce protein in this way is a luxury that can hardly be justified given the current world food situation.

Thus, for the purposes of the model, it is supposed that animals are only fed on pasture — land not appropriate for agricultural use — and with a part of the nonedible part of agricultural production. This last source of forage is not exploited sufficiently in many regions of the world.

Inputs to Animal Production — International data on factors and inputs specifically for animal production are very scarce, because many cannot be distinguished from those used for agricultural purposes. Also, animal production contributes a very low proportion of the total production of calories and proteins, and it is assumed that this situation will continue throughout the time horizon of the model. Therefore, it was decided to treat animal production more simply than agricultural production. The global cost of an increase in animal production has been calculated, and it is assumed that such production should grow linearly as economic resources permit, up to a limit imposed by natural and agricultural constraints.

Maximum Animal Production — The maximum animal production for a given year depends, in the model, on two factors: the capacity of grazing land (a fixed parameter in the model) and the production of agricultural subproducts not suitable for human consumption.

The efficiency of animals in converting forage into meat varies according to the type of animal and forage used. In the model, aggregated production of meat is estimated to take place at 15% efficiency.

Animal production is, of course, also affected by losses in processing, storage, and transportation. As in the case of agricultural products, it is assumed that the loss decreases in underdeveloped countries until it reaches, at the end of 20 years, the value reached in the more advanced countries.

Figure 14 is a flowchart of the animal production subsector.

Fisheries

In 1970, freshwater fishing accounted for only about 12% of the total world catch. The total catch (fresh and sea fish) in 1970 was taken from FAO statistics.

The procedure used in this subsector was essentially the same as that applied for animal production. Costs estimated by FAO for fisheries in each region were divided by the caloric content of extra fish caught, giving an approximation of the cost per unit of increased fish production.

It is assumed that fish production increases up to a certain limit, at a rate determined by the economic resources available. Losses in processing, transportation, etc., are estimated to be about 17% and are considered to be the same for all regions and over time.

Maximum Fish Production — There are many estimates of the maximum possible fish catch. The model uses the FAO calculation of 120 million tonnes (live weight) for sea fish, crustaceans, and mollusks, excluding whales. This

Table 6. Estimates of the maximum possible fish production (10^{12} Kcal/year).

Developed countries	74.6
Latin America	15.2
Asia	24.2
Africa	6.0
Total	120.0

figure is lower than others available and only includes currently preferred species.

The most difficult problem consists in establishing the maximum production for each region in the model, and to do this it was necessary to make some assumptions. Based on the analysis of studies by Ryther, it was assumed that potential world fish production in each region is proportional to the area of continental shelf around it. Estimates are given in Table 6.

Figure 15 is a flowchart for the fish production subsector.

Levels of Nutrition

In the model, it is assumed that a basic level of nutrition of 3000 calories and 100 grams of protein is required per person per day. As is well known, food requirements vary with climate, age, and weight of individuals, etc. It was decided, however, to use the above figures as global averages, because of the difficulty in incorporating a more detailed breakdown of requirements given the high level of geographic aggregation in the model. Tests with preliminary runs show that the results of the model in the long and medium term varied very little when different values were used for different regions.

Figure 16 shows the structure and operation of the food sector. The optimization process enables the manpower and capital required in the sector to be calculated and, from the production function, the gross product can be obtained. The difference between this value and that of the previous year is the net addition to the total product of the sector, and this, in turn, is shared between the agricultural subsector, livestock, and fisheries. By means of a simple linear programing calculation, the arable product is divided into two parts, one to develop new land and another to produce more fertilizers (and other inputs), so as to maximize yield per hectare. From the three subsectors, it is possible to calculate the total quantity of calories and protein reaching the market and the per capita consumption.

69

Chapter 7

Housing and Urbanization

The provision of housing, unlike food production, is not subject to problems caused by physical limits. Material with which houses are built, or could be built, are abundant and can be found almost anywhere in the world. Also, given the enormous variety of materials and technologies that can be used, houses can generally be built with predominantly local materials, thus reducing to a minimum the need for transportation over long distances.

However, housing construction does not depend exclusively on the availability of suitable raw materials. These materials have to be extracted and require a certain degree of preparation, however small; auxiliary installations, such as sanitary fixtures, require the development of sizeable industries. Given the existing housing deficit, which is described in detail later, housing construction requires a large investment per person, which implies an enormous strain on the precarious economies of underdeveloped countries.

The questions that must be answered in the housing sector are essentially the following: what is the type of housing that, although compatible with the material available in poor countries, fulfills the minimum conditions for it to be considered adequate? In what period can the various regions eliminate the housing deficit and provide an adequate dwelling for each family, bearing in mind that at the same time deficits in other basic needs must be met?

It must also be remembered that it is not enough to build houses; they also require infrastructure services — sewerage, drinking water, energy, access roads, etc. — that all contribute to making them genuinely habitable.

In a society like that proposed in the model, rural and urban areas would be harmoniously integrated; differences that arise naturally from their different functions in the production system should not imply inequalities regarding general well-being and opportunities for personal fulfillment.

To achieve this objective within the framework of the social and political changes being proposed, one of the fundamental measures must be to encourage the settlement of the rural population into groups of a certain size. Apart from the social and psychosocial advantages — more personal interaction, increased community spirit, political participation, etc. — it is the only economic means of providing adequate basic services such as education, hygiene, and transportation to the population.

The particular form that the urban–rural distribution will take in each region or country would be determined by the production structure, which in turn would be conditioned by the sociopolitical system. Thus only very general reference is made here to the characteristics that this structure should have; but, before dealing with this, the housing problem (which is intimately linked to the production structure) will be considered.

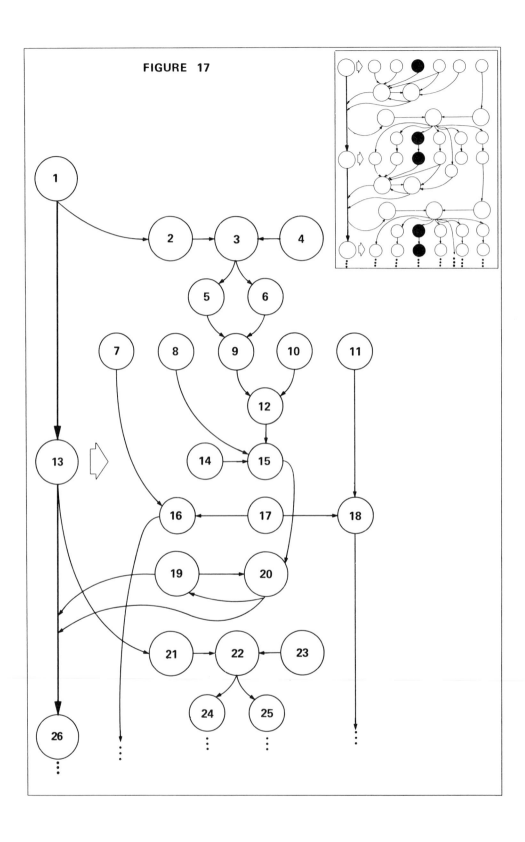

FIGURE 17

Housing

The Housing Deficit — In spite of deficiencies in the statistics, it is estimated that between 50 and 60% of the population of the world live in houses that are to some extent unsatisfactory; they are poorly constructed, inadequately equipped, excessively crowded together, or in unacceptable environmental conditions. If the population of the world is put at 3600 million in 1970, between 1800 and 2200 million people live in houses of varying degrees of deterioration and deficiency in basic services. The true situation, however, can be appreciated more easily from the following data on the persons affected in different regions:

(*a*) eight of every 10 inhabitants in the rural areas of developing countries (i.e. 1500 million from a total of some 1900 million);

(*b*) of urban areas in developing countries, one in two inhabitants (320 million of a total of 650 million);

(*c*) in developed countries, two in every 10 inhabitants of rural areas (75 million of a total of 370 million); and

(*d*) in the urban areas of developed countries, two in every 10 inhabitants (140 million out of a total of 720 million).

In summary, some 2060 million persons lack adequate housing.[10]

If these estimates are correct, then, taking the division of the world used in the model, the housing deficit for each region is as follows: developed countries 7%; Latin America 40%; Africa 60%; Asia and Australasia 50%.

Housing in the Proposed Society

Cost of Housing — If it is to be effective, a plan to deal with the problem of housing in the world must take account of the needs of the sector, allowing for growth of the population, the need to overcome current deficiencies, and finally, the replacement of obsolete houses. An assessment of the possibility of carrying through such a plan requires estimates of the cost of housing, and so of total investment required.

---

[10]These figures are calculated from estimates from publications put out by individual countries and on-the-spot studies by those working on the sector. They are considerably higher than the more generally accepted estimates published by international organizations.

Fig. 17. Operation of the urbanization and housing sector during optimization.

1 Total population	14 Family size
2 Total labour 1980	15 Houses per family
3 Optimization	16 Urbanization rate 1981
4 Total capital 1980	17 New houses
5 Labour in urbanization & housing	18 Housing stock 1981
6 Capital in urbanization & housing	19 Life expectancy
7 Rate of urbanization	20 Birthrate
8 Square metres per capita	21 Total labour 1981
9 Production function	22 Optimization
10 Building cost per m²	23 Total capital 1981
11 Housing stock 1980	24 Labour in housing & urbanization
12 Square metres built in 1981	25 Capital in housing & urbanization
13 Total population 1980	26 Total population 1981

In the model, the cost of 1 square metre of housing has been set at U.S. $35 (1960) in the underdeveloped regions (Asia, Latin America, and Africa). Although this cost is somewhat lower than current costs in some underdeveloped countries, it is sufficient for the construction of two bedrooms, one kitchen–dining room, one living room, and one toilet and washroom. The total cost of such a dwelling is $1750.

Because their average standards are so much higher, the minimum dwelling in the model for the developed countries has an area of 70 square metres for an average family of 3.5 people. The cost of construction is estimated to be $4900 ($70 per square metre).

Although the costs used in the model for underdeveloped and developed areas might seem low in comparison with current costs, it is thought that they are realistic, and might be reduced even further, for the following reasons:

(a) Social ownership of the land, apart from its influence on cost, will put an end to useless subdivisions, making a more rational distribution of land possible. The consequences would be an increase in the efficiency of the infrastructural services, a reduction in administrative costs, and the possibility of planning standardized groups of dwellings.

(b) The low productivity in construction could be improved by standardized techniques and patterns for construction, organization, etc.

(c) The building industry offers a wide range of possibilities for technological research. The use of local materials could be one of the most important factors in the production costs.

The adoption of a standard dwelling in the model obviously does not mean that existing differences in climate, cultural habits, availability of local raw materials for construction, and so on, should be ignored. For operational reasons and the lack of data, it was necessary to simplify the basic assumption in the model. Within the established cost limit, there is ample scope for varying the type of house according to the local conditions.

The cost of the standard dwelling in each region represents only a point of reference that is compatible with current economic conditions. As soon as the model indicates that an economy has reached a degree of development that enables it to satisfy all basic needs, a part of its product is then channeled into the improvement of the type of housing.

The Concept of Urbanization in the Model

As already stated with reference to the demographic sector, urbanization has a direct influence on some of the demographic variables. In particular, it tends to increase life expectancy and to decrease infant mortality. The main indirect effect is a reduction in birthrate and hence in the rate of population growth.

The United Nations defines an urban population as one that contains more than a certain number of inhabitants. Although the minimum varies considerably from country to country, the most generally accepted figure is 20000 inhabitants. Initial data on urban population in the model are taken from United Nations statistics, and are therefore based on their criteria.

The effect of urbanization on life expectancy and infant mortality is due not merely to the fact of people living in cities of a certain size, but to the fact that, in cities, particularly in less developed countries, basic services such as education, health, and drinking water are more readily available.

74

For this reason, together with the social and psychological factors mentioned earlier, the model assumes that any housing built from the moment optimization begins *is built as part of a group*. This applies to new dwellings, built either in response to the existing deficit, or to further population growth, as well as to housing built to replace obsolete buildings (it is assumed that the average life of a house is 70 years).

The number of houses in a group must be at least the minimum necessary to provide community services, such as education and health. As stated above, the new houses would include sanitary facilities and would be linked to the water system and to sewerage networks. Therefore, in the model, *all new housing is considered to be urban* because of the quality of, and access to, services, something that has been far more evident in relatively large cities.

Figure 17 describes the operation of the sector in the optimization phase. The process of optimization involves the calculation of the manpower and capital allocated to the sector, and the gross sectoral product is derived using a production function. The difference between the product of one year and that of the previous year makes it possible to calculate, knowing costs, the total number of square metres of housing that can be produced. (Costs change in underdeveloped regions after basic needs are fulfilled, as explained earlier.) The demographic sector provides the average family size and total population, thus giving the total number of families. Each year a number of square metres is allocated per person, which enables calculation of the number and average size of buildings that could be built. Knowing the stock of the previous year, it is possible to find how many families have adequate housing. The rate of urbanization can also be calculated, assuming that all buildings constructed after 1980 are urban. The rate of urbanization reduces the amount of potentially arable land: it is assumed that 50% of new buildings will be on land suitable for agriculture.

Chapter 8

Education

Education is represented by a separate sector for two main reasons: first, because it is assumed to be of fundamental importance for the attainment of the desired society, and, secondly, because education is considered to be one of the basic requirements once such a society has been achieved.

One of the central premises in the model is the possibility of moving the world in the direction of an ideal. This implies looking at history as a dynamic and open process; it is not a predetermined unfolding of a story, but is dependent on the actions of men. In the last analysis, these actions are the determinants of history and society.

This view assigns a significant role to education, and leads us to include it as one of the central variables of the model. The importance attributed to the influence of education derives from the belief that it is a prerequisite for generating a society composed of active, useful, participating individuals and groups.

In other words, it is considered that, first, education can be an instrument for social change. From the perspective of the individual, it provides an opportunity for creating the capacity required for participation in producing changes and obtaining the benefits derived from the new situation. The results presented in Chapter 5 reinforce this argument; they show that education is one of the most influential factors on demographic evolution, and particularly on life expectancy. Secondly, education is considered to be a basic and permanent need of individuals. To conceive education as a basic need thoughout an individual's lifetime implies the adoption of a perspective that is rather different from the traditional one, not only with regard to the individual process but also in relation to the social actions required to satisfy these needs.

Permanent Education: A New View of Education

To participate in producing changes, to live a full life, requires permanent education. When change is broad and rapid, most of the human behavioural resources rapidly become "out-of-date" and lose their operative efficiency in all (or almost all) spheres of activity.

The concept of change as a result of deliberate action, and not as some kind of spontaneous happening, also suggests a revision of the traditional view of the function of education. It suggests that it is necessary to give up the idea of education as a means of adapting people to fit in with society as given, and to start thinking of it as an aid to help people participate in their society and its evolution.

The scope of education is limited in the model to organized, formal training, although this is to underestimate its true breadth and significance.

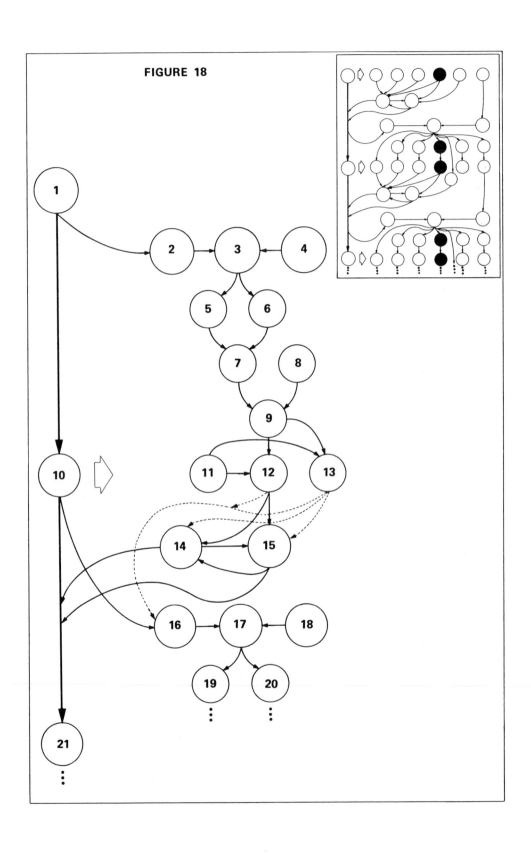

FIGURE 18

From different perspectives, the total scope of education can include:

(1) *School* and *extramural* education.

(2) *Initial* and *"post-experience"* education.

(3) *Formal* education (corresponding to the different levels and modalities of the school system), *nonformal* (which focuses on the acquisition of specific personal capabilities to apply in domestic, social, economic, political, or cultural life), and *informal* education (which leads to personal growth and enrichment).

(4) *Institutionalized* education and *independent* education (the latter being marginally associated with the institutional sphere).

(5) *Direct* or face-to-face education, and *indirect* or "at-a-distance" education (the latter carried out using various technological resources).

The preceding outline indicates the possibility of making education a normal activity for people throughout their lives. This requires that all the population has the necessary capacity and competence to manage their education in an autonomous way; this is one of the key factors in the educational system being advocated.

To face this problem, it is necessary to reconsider the prevailing requirements for the basic education received at school, because this is intended to provide the starting point for the personal expansion of "education" just indicated. Because of this, it is proposed to replace the present assessment criteria for education by a concept we call the *"point of educational autonomy."* This is defined as the achievement of that basic threshold of autonomy and self-sufficiency that is needed for a satisfactory and efficient performance in the decisions, planning, and control of education at the individual, as well as the group, level.

The Minimum Levels of Education

In accordance with the philosophy of the model, these paragraphs describe the minimum levels of education that are considered indispensable for satisfying individual and social needs.

The desirable levels are grouped into four categories:

(1) *Basic education*, from the age of six (98% of the age-group), oriented to the achievement of the point of educational autonomy. It is thought that this standard can be reached with between 8 and 12 years of schooling (a maximum of 12 years is used in the model).

Fig. 18. Operation of the education sector during optimization.

1 Total population	12 Initial enrollment rate
2 Labour force 1980	13 Continuous education: incorporation rate
3 Optimization	14 Life expectancy at birth
4 Total capital 1980	15 Birthrate
5 Education labour force	16 Total labour force 1981
6 Education capital	17 Optimization
7 Production function	18 Total capital 1981
8 Cost	19 Education labour force
9 Macrosystem: education places	20 Education capital
10 Total population 1980	21 Total population 1981
11 Age structure	

(2) *Middle and high-level education oriented to training a critical mass of middle and higher staff.* The social necessity of skilled human resources requires that a certain proportion of the population receive a middle and high level training to equip them for specific economic, social, and political activity, as well as for autonomous and self-sustained scientific, technological, and "cultural" development. It is not unreasonable to assume that at least 7% of the total population undertake medium-level studies and 2% higher education as a first stage.

(3) *Continuing education.* All the adult population between the ages of 20 and 50 will have 3 years of education (1:10 of their active life, which is estimated to be 30 years). This will be divided into 30 modules, each the equivalent of 6 weeks full-time education.

This scheme would permit services to be provided for about 12% of the population in the middle age-group at any given time. The object of having continuous education available to the adult population is to provide opportunities for retraining or updating, advancing, or enlarging on previous educational achievements or qualifications. This could be organized according to the needs emerging in various areas (work, politics, community, domestic or cultural life), or according to the desires, aspirations, or interests for personal fulfillment, expression, or expansion.

(4) *Compensatory education.* Until the target of initial basic education is reached, it will be necessary to provide education to compensate that part of the adult population that was not able to obtain the minimum level. This compensatory action would attempt to ensure that all adults lacking education reach the minimum standard proposed for the initial education of the young, namely, the point of educational autonomy.

The minimum level proposed and that currently existing can only be compared in terms of formal schooling, which is mainly for the young. There are no data available on a world scale for either extramural education or for adult education in general, except for the illiteracy rate and the records of some literacy campaigns.

UNESCO data show that the advanced countries already have universal primary education. In the less developed regions, the enrollment rate for primary education is substantially lower: in Latin America 75%; Africa 40%; and Asia 55%. Furthermore, early leaving is particularly high in several regions (especially in their rural areas); the rate of early leaving for Africa and Latin America is around 55–60% and, in both regions, a quarter of the registered children repeat the first year. Also, in Asia and Africa, there is a sharp inequality in the sex distribution of registrations.

According to UNESCO, in 1970 nearly one-third of the total world population over 15 was illiterate (in Africa 74%; Asia 47%; and Latin America 24%). The high level of illiteracy provides an indication of the gap between the desired and the present situations.

Qualitative Aspects of Education

To achieve the satisfaction of the minimal needs of education only in quantitative terms would imply not only a partial response to the problem but, rather, a response that is contradictory to the basic premises of the model. It is a question of providing better education to more people for a longer period of time, but it is also a question of a qualitative change in the present context of education.

The following are the principal characteristics, in relation to quality, that define the type of education proposed: (1) prospective orientation; (2) individual and social relevance; (3) orientation toward the nation and the world outside; (4) fostering efficiency in the skills required for communication; (5) orientation toward the achievement of a common quality of life; (6) orientation toward a liberating education; (7) being directed toward equality of opportunity.

Formalization of the Sector

At the start of the model (1960), data regarding the rate of registration for 6- to 18-year-olds are used, together with the proportion of GNP allocated to education. The annual average cost per student is calculated in the way described in Chapter 4.

In subsequent years, given the capital available and the sectoral labour force, the production function can be used to calculate the gross product allocated to the sector. With this data, and knowing the average cost of educating one student, the number of places available in the education system is calculated. Then, from the age structure given by the demographic subsystem, the population between 6 and 18 years is known, so that the registration rate can be calculated.

When the registration rate reaches 98%, the cost per student is incremented at an accumulative annual rate of 2% in the three least developed regions, until a maximum of U.S. $150 is reached. This figure can be modified, but it is thought that it is large enough to achieve levels of quality in education that are similar to those in the advanced countries. A certain proportion of this increase is devoted to improving the quality in other educational categories included in the sector, although evaluation of these educational levels is not included in the results of the model.

Figure 18 indicates the behaviour of the sector. The dotted line shows the effect of education on the participation rate of the labour force. This effect is undoubtedly significant, but research into it, and into other variables thought to be significant, has started only recently. Thus it has not been incorporated into the model.

81

Chapter 9

The Physical Feasibility of the Proposed Society

The mathematical model that has been described was built to test the physical viability of the proposed society. Essentially this involved determining the period of time needed and the conditions under which the different regions could satisfy basic needs to given levels. It was also designed to examine the effects of the proposed policies on demographic variables.

The standard, or basic, run is described below. Using its results as a starting point, other runs were made to explore the effects of various modifications of the model.

The assumptions and the main characteristics of the standard run are as follows:

(a) The levels required for satisfaction of basic needs, such as food and education, are incorporated in the respective subsystems (3000 calories and 100 grams of protein per person per day; 12 years of basic education between the ages of 7 and 18). For advanced countries, the caloric level was fixed at 3200, bearing in mind that in 1970 the average intake in these countries had already reached 3063.

Regarding housing in advanced countries and Latin America, the target of one house per family is used. This house is of the type described in Chapter 7.

For Africa and Asia, although the final objective remains the same, the "standard" house was initially taken to be more modest. In these two regions, given the current desperate situation in housing and complementary services, the cost of the "standard" house is much higher than the average cost of existing houses. For this reason, it was decided that it would be best to begin by considering houses that were cheaper and smaller than the desired house. Houses with 7 square metres per person were considered at a cost of U.S. $23.40 per square metre in Africa, and U.S. $11.20 in Asia. These costs were calculated bearing in mind the minimum area needed per person to avoid crowding and using the economic capabilities of the regions in 1970 as a basis. At that time the real costs per square metre were U.S. $16.40 for Africa, and U.S. $7.80 for Asia. Thus the values taken in the model are higher than the actual costs.

Housing conditions in Africa and Asia gradually improve and reach the developing countries' target area and quality in 20 years.

Once all the basic needs are satisfied, it is possible to improve education and housing. In the case of housing, the area and cost per person are increased, so that, in 40 years, it is possible to build houses similar to those in developed countries.

The maximum housing standard was fixed at 1.5 units per family in all regions. This would be reflected by larger areas being covered, better

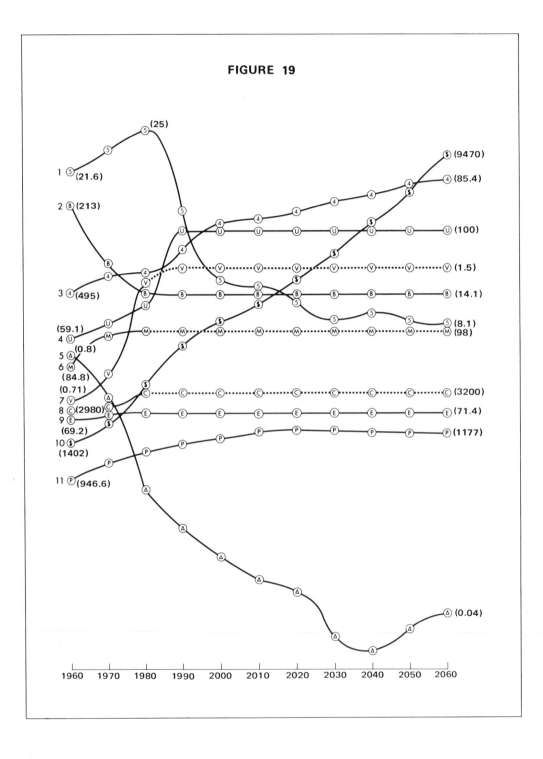

FIGURE 19

building materials, recreational facilities, etc.

The annual cost of education per student in underdeveloped countries is increased at a compounded annual rate of 2% to a maximum of U.S. $150, starting when all basic needs have been satisfied. The additional investment is used to improve the quality of education and educational facilities.

In the population submodel, housing has no further influence on the birthrate after the target of one house for every four persons has been reached; this conclusion was reached after studying statistics for 121 countries.

(b) An aggregated yield of 4 tonnes per hectare per year (10^7 Kcal/ha·yr) is assumed in agriculture (see Chapter 6). Once the desired per capita level of proteins and calories is reached, a stock of food reserves is built up. The volume of reserves depends on the economic potential of the region and on the competing demand for resources for the other basic needs.

(c) Manpower: see Chapter 4. In the runs, the optimization mechanism transfers manpower from one sector of the economy to another, but the rate of transfer can never exceed 2% of the manpower in any sector in a particular year.

(d) The allocation of capital to sectors remains constant between 1960 and 1980. Agricultural manpower diminishes in accordance with ILO data and is proportionally transferred to other sectors. From 1980 this distribution is determined by the optimization technique.

(e) Technological progress: see Chapter 4.

(f) The maximum rate of investment was fixed at 25%. This constraint is based on historical experience and on the consideration of social factors. This upper limit is not absolute, however; if a situation arises in which the constraints are incompatible with one another, any can be relaxed in the optimization process, with the exception of the transfer of labour and capital from sector to sector, following a preestablished order of priorities.

(g) The percentage of GNP allocated to sector 4 (other services and consumer goods) should not fall below 45% of total production, nor must it increase with respect to its 1970 level until basic needs are satisfied. The reasons for imposing these two restrictions are as follows.

The first is based on the fact that, during the period in which basic needs are not satisfied, it might be necessary to restrict nonessential consumption. In sector 4, however, there are many goods and services that are essential — infrastructure, clothing, administration and government, education other than basic, etc. — and others that are not indispensable. Analysis of the sector has led to the conclusion that approximately 45% is the minimum percentage compatible with adequate operation of the economy. The second restriction is imposed because it is not reasonable to

---

Fig. 19. Time period and conditions required for developing countries to satisfy basic needs to given levels.

1 Percentage of GNP allocated to sector 5 (5)
2 Birthrate (B)
3 Percentage of GNP allocated to sector 4 (4)
4 Urbanization (U)
5 Population growth rate (△)
6 Enrollment (M)

7 Houses per family (V)
8 Total calories (C)
9 Life expectancy (E)
10 GNP per capita in dollars ($)
11 Total population (P)

consider increasing the relative importance of sector 4 while a part of the population has still not had its basic needs satisfied.

In the runs of the model, the evolution of sector 4 can be considered to be an indicator of the general level of well-being achieved, over and above basic needs.

(h) In developed regions, when GNP per capita exceeds U.S. $4500, annual economic growth is restricted between 1 and 2% in accordance with the criteria established in Chapter 2. This leads to both a decrease in the rate of investment and an increase in the proportion of GNP allocated to sector 4. For the underdeveloped regions, once basic needs are satisfied, the growth rate in GNP per capita has to be at least 2%. The object of this differential growth rate is to gradually reduce the gap between the developed and underdeveloped regions.

(i) One of the indicators used in the model, and used in the figures illustrating the runs, is GNP per capita. However, the GNP figures quoted cannot be directly compared with real figures because all the values given in the model are expressed in 1960 dollars. As the prices of different goods vary in real economies, a general price index that does not appear in the model is used to convert prices to 1960 dollars. Thus, in the model, GNP per capita is measured in "real" terms.

In presenting the results, the most important and revealing indicators about socioeconomic evolution of the regions are described; the model provides much additional data on economics, population, food, etc., that are not included for reasons of simplicity and ease of comprehension.

When referring to diagrams, note that the scales used are different in each case. The highest and the lowest values of variables are given, thus making possible comparisons between regions.

In interpreting results, it should be stressed that the dates are not intended to be precise. They indicate the approximate time periods needed for the achievement of certain objectives. The results of this run, for each region, are described below.

Table 7. Evolution of the main economic and demographic and health indicators for developed countries.

	1960	1980	2000	2020	2040	2060
Economic indicators						
GNP/capita	1402	2962	4778	5984	7512	9470
Investment rate (% GNP)	21.6	25	11.9	10.2	9.2	8.1
Consumption (% GNP)	49.5	55.6	70.9	75.0	80.5	85.4
% GNP allocated to food	16.7	8.69	8.03	6.7	4.13	2.52
Demographic and health indicators						
Population growth rate (%)	1.3	0.41	0.22	0.03	−0.05	0.04
Total population (*millions*)	947	1082	1150	1181	1175	1177
Life expectancy (*years*)	69.2	71.15	71.20	71.24	71.33	71.4
Crude mortality rate	10.8	10.2	11.7	13.85	14.6	13.65
Birthrate	21.3	14.2	14.11	14.1	14.05	14.08
Infant mortality	26.6	21.58	21.30	21.20	20.99	20.87
Persons/family	3.7	3.4	3	2.84	2.8	2.86

Developed Countries — Predictably, bearing in mind the initial conditions, basic needs are satisfied in the first few years of the run (Fig. 19) in developed countries.

At the end of the run, with population stabilized, 27% of potentially cultivatable land remains unused. Moreover, from the late 1980s onward, the developed countries keep a stock of food equivalent to 1 year's consumption.

Life expectancy, which was 69.2 years in 1960, increases to 70.5 by the end of the 1970s and to 71.4 years by the end of the run.

As can also be seen in Fig. 19, GNP per capita grows from U.S. $1402 in 1960 to U.S. $4500 in 1995. From that year onward, the growth rate decreases, with GNP per capita reaching U.S. $9470 in the year 2060.

Sector 4 absorbs 48.5% of output in 1960 rising to 85.4% in 2060. The rate of investment goes down from 21.6% in 1960 to only 8.1% in 2060.

A very useful indicator of the level of well-being is provided by the proportion of GNP spent on food; in advanced countries, this proportion decreases from 16.7% in 1960 to 2.5% in 2060.

In Table 7 the evolution of the main economic and demographic and health indicators is given.

The population growth rate, which was 1.3% in 1960, is reduced to zero by 2023; by 2047 it becomes slightly negative, after which it again increases; the population remains essentially constant. These fluctuations around zero population growth are due to the mortality rate, which varies in relation to the population pyramid.

The evolution of the main demographic indicators is shown in Fig. 19 and Table 7.

The advanced countries can reach high levels of well-being even if their economic growth rate is drastically reduced in the future, i.e., they have the opportunity of reducing work, and increasing leisure time, while maintaining a growth rate that will allow them to preserve and continuously improve the physical and human environment.

Latin America — The general evolution of Latin America, if the proposed policies are applied, would make it possible to fulfill the basic needs in the early 1990s (Fig. 20). Regarding food, it would be necessary to develop relatively little extra land for agricultural purposes. The proportion of uncultivated land in 1960 was 83.5%, and in the year 2060 this would only be reduced to 63.2%. Before the turn of the century it would already be possible to have a stock of food sufficient for 1 year, and that level is maintained until 2060.

The GNP per capita rises from U.S. $372 in 1960 to U.S. $5746 at the end of the run. The satisfaction of basic needs can be achieved with a GNP of U.S. $809.

In sector 4, consumption rises from 49.6% of output in 1960 to 61.6% in 2060, and the rate of investment from 18.2% in 1960 to 25% in 1986, this value being maintained until the end of the run, so that housing, education, and general living conditions could be improved in order to close the gap between this region and the developed countries.

In Fig. 20 and Table 8, the evolution of the main economic and demographic and health indicators is shown.

It is perhaps the population figures that show the most interesting results. The growth rate, which was 2.8% in 1960, decreases as general

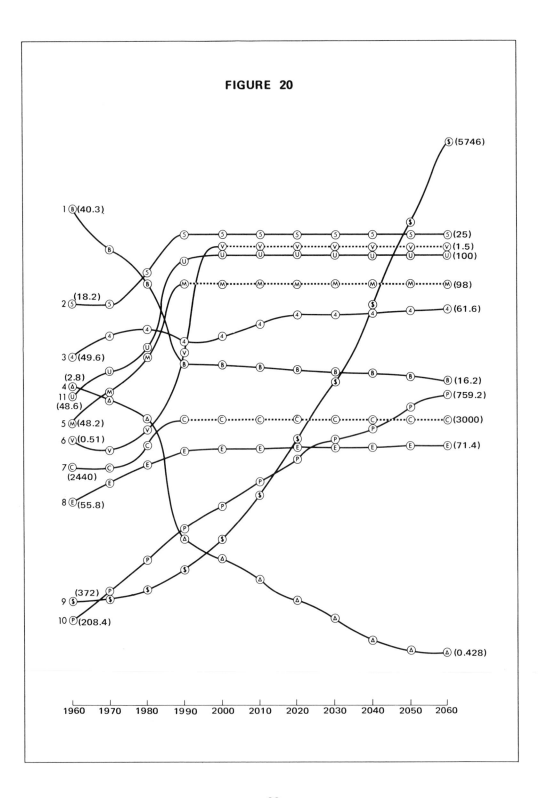

FIGURE 20

Table 8. Evolution of the main economic and demographic and health indicators for Latin America.

	1960	1980	2000	2020	2040	2060
Economic indicators						
GNP/capita	372	530	1107	2247	3822	5746
Investment rate (% *GNP*)	18.2	21.2	25	25	25	25
Consumption (% *GNP*)	49.6	55.8	54.8	59.8	60.6	61.6
% GNP allocated to food	21.2	14.21	10.63	7.69	6.3	5.34
Demographic and health indicators						
Population growth rate (%)	2.8	2.6	1.27	0.89	0.56	0.43
Total population (*millions*)	208.4	350.6	486.3	601.2	693.9	759.2
Life expectancy (*years*)	55.8	65.8	70.24	20.75	71.04	71.38
Crude mortality rate	14.7	7.02	5.91	8.53	11.56	12.03
Birthrate	40.36	30.04	18.34	17.57	17.07	16.22
Infant mortality	115	37	24	22.5	21.7	20.88
Persons/family	4.5	4.9	3.5	3.3	3.1	3

well-being improves, and reaches 1.27% at the beginning of the next century and 0.43% by the year 2060; population stabilization is therefore approached. Total population rises from 208.4 million in 1960 to 759 million in 2060.

In conclusion, Latin America could adequately satisfy the basic needs of the whole population within one generation from the implementation of the proposed policies. Subsequently, Latin America could improve its general level of well-being as indicated by the increasing proportion of sector 4 to total output.

Africa — Africa also satisfies its basic needs, but in a longer time period than Latin America, the target being reached in 2008. Figure 21 shows the main demographic and socioeconomic indicators.

Food reserves reach a maximum of 8 months at the beginning of the next century, and subsequently, owing to the need to allocate more resources to education and housing, they begin to decrease to a level of just over 1 month by 2060.

From 2016, the economic capacity exists to achieve the equivalent of 1.5 houses per family and to improve continuously the quality of the housing.

It is worth restating the differences taken for housing targets in the basic needs function between regions. Although the final number of houses per family is equal in all regions, the quality of the housing is different. In developed countries the starting point is a stock of houses similar to the type

---

Fig. 20. Time period and conditions required for Latin America to satisfy basic needs to given levels.

1 Birthrate (B)	7 Total calories (C)
2 Percentage of GNP allocated to sector 5 (5)	8 Life expectancy (E)
3 Percentage of GNP allocated to sector 4 (4)	9 GNP per capita in 1960 dollars ($)
4 Population growth rate (△)	10 Total population (P)
5 Enrollment (M)	11 Urbanization (U)
6 Houses per family (V)	

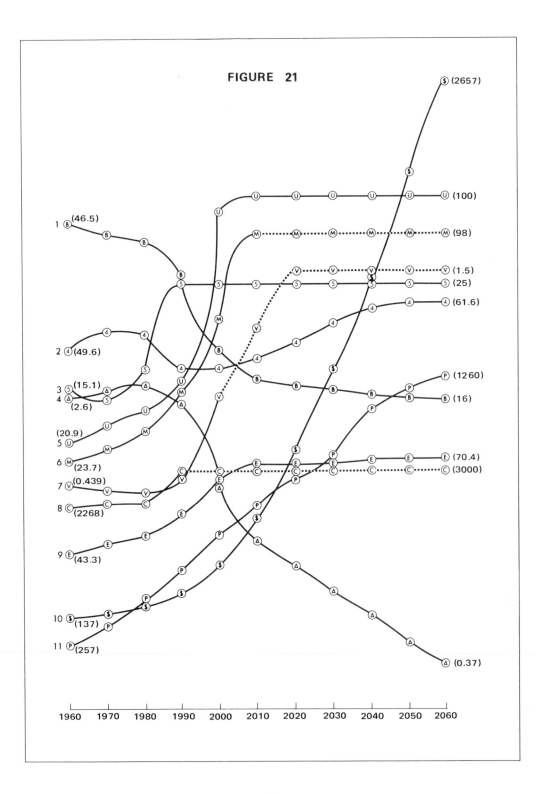

FIGURE 21

Table 9. Evolution of the main economic and demographic and health indicators for Africa.

	1960	1980	2000	2020	2040	2060
Economic indicators						
GNP/capita	137	167	387	911	1728	2657
Investment rate (% GNP)	15.1	16.7	25	25	25	25
Consumption (% GNP)	49.6	53.9	45.4	51.6	59.6	61.6
% GNP allocated to food	26.40	22.16	20	14.29	7.27	4.86
Demographic and health indicators						
Population growth rate (%)	2.6	2.69	1.93	1.19	0.79	0.37
Total population (*millions*)	257	432.4	701.5	929.2	1127	1260
Life expectancy (*years*)	43.4	48.4	64.6	68.8	70	70.4
Crude mortality rate	20.6	17.04	7.14	6.85	9.28	12.4
Infant mortality	196	163	39.9	27.4	24.4	23.2
Birthrate	46.5	42.8	24.6	18.7	17.1	16
Persons/family	4.5	4.7	4	3.5	3.3	3

established as the initial target, and a good infrastructure of services exists. Therefore, the progress reflected in the figure of 1.5 houses per family means that a large proportion of the houses are of a considerably higher standard than the target house for the region. In the underdeveloped countries, particularly in Asia and Africa, the existence of a stock of very deficient housing means that at the end of the run, the average quality of housing will still be considerably below the level achieved by the developed countries.

At the end of the run, in 2060, the proportion of uncultivated land is still very high (49%).

Life expectancy increases continuously from the initial level of 43.3 years in 1960, to 70.4 years by the end of the run.

GNP per capita, U.S. $137 in 1960, reaches U.S. $559 in 2008, when all basic needs are satisfied, and reaches U.S. $2657 in the last year of the run. The proportion of GNP allocated to consumption rises from 49.6% in 1960 to 61.6% in 2060.

The proportion of GNP allocated to food decreases steadily from 26.4% in 1960 to 4.86% at the end of the run.

Table 9 shows the evolution of the main economic and demographic and health indicators.

Therefore, it is possible to say that if the policies proposed are applied, Africa can satisfy the basic needs of its population within 30 years, starting from 1980, and thereafter can improve its general level of well-being substantially.

Fig. 21. Time period and conditions required for Africa to satisfy basic needs to given levels.

1 Birthrate (B)
2 Percentage of GNP allocated to sector 4 (4)
3 Percentage of GNP allocated to sector 5 (5)
4 Population growth rate (△)
5 Urbanization (U)
6 Enrollment (M)
7 Houses per family (V)
8 Total calories (C)
9 Life expectancy (E)
10 GNP per capita in 1960 dollars ($)
11 Total population (P)

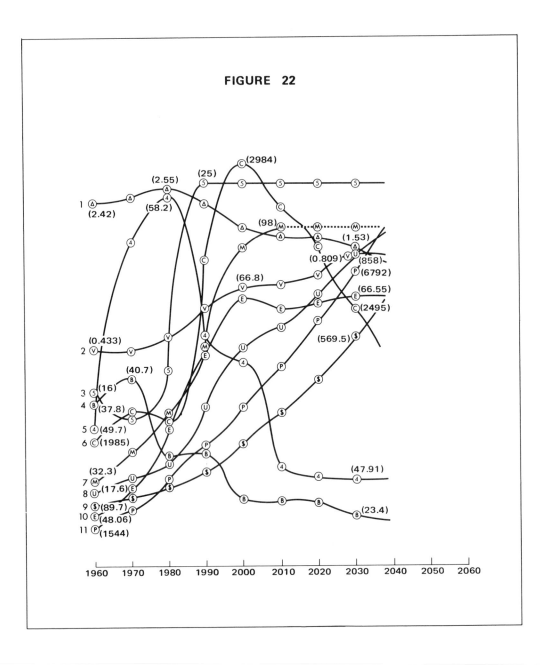

FIGURE 22

Fig. 22. Time period and conditions required for Asia to satisfy basic needs to given levels.

1 Population growth rate (△)
2 Houses per family (V)
3 Percentage of GNP allocated to sector 5 (5)
4 Birthrate (B)
5 Percentage of GNP allocated to sector 4 (4)
6 Total calories (C)

7 Enrollment (M)
8 Urbanization (U)
9 GNP per capita in 1960 dollars ($)
10 Life expectancy (E)
11 Total population (P)

Asia — The results of the run for Asia are very different from the results for other regions because basic needs are not satisfied to the desired levels (Fig. 22).

In the food sector, a consumption rate of 2800 calories per person per day is achieved by 1992, and that level is maintained until the mid-2020s. It declines slowly after that and in 2040 reaches almost the same level as in 1960 (2150 calories). Thereafter the decline accelerates until levels are reached that are incompatible with survival. In the housing sector, the desired levels are not achieved either, but there is a noticeable improvement, with the level reaching 0.82 houses per family in 2040. Education is the only basic need that is totally satisfied by the year 2040.

Table 10 shows the evolution of the main economic and demographic and health indicators.

The failure to attain the satisfaction of basic needs to the desired levels is reflected in the demographic indicators (Table 10). The rate of population growth is reduced very slowly, and the population increases fivefold in 80 years, reaching 7840 million in 2040. Life expectancy at birth improves, but is always below levels in other regions. Also, infant mortality does not compare favourably with Latin America and Africa. The runs were stopped at the year 2040 because after that date the indicators (particularly life expectancy) cease to have any meaning. Although the calories provided by the food sector drop below the minimum required for survival, life expectancy remains relatively high owing to the effects of education and housing; the function that links life expectancy to the socioeconomic variables is continuous, and no minimum value for food intake was established below which this indicator is reduced to zero.

The life expectancy function is meaningful only when food intake is adequate to keep a person alive and to allow levels of physical activity that currently exist in the poorest societies.

The problem in Asia arises in the food sector. By 2010, all available land is being cultivated. Thereafter, economic effort in the sector is devoted to increasing livestock and fisheries. This, however, is not enough to feed the growing population adequately, and consumption drops rapidly to below the minimum needed for survival.

The rapid increase in the cost of producing food, due to the development of new land for agriculture, takes resources from the rest of the economy, causing backwardness and also hindering the satisfaction of the other basic needs. In summary, the delay in reaching adequate levels of well-being leads to a sustained high population growth rate, and a vicious circle develops: increased population and the increased cost of producing food make it more and more difficult to satisfy basic needs.

Nevertheless, the problem of Asia is not a case of absolute limits, because the other regions still have great expanses of uncultivated land when their populations have become stable. Asia could import food, but, for reasons already explained in the food sector, this solution is only acceptable as a last resort.

An obvious solution to the problem could be to try to raise agricultural yields, which are still well below the maximum theoretical levels. To test this hypothesis, a run was made assuming that Asia manages to raise agricultural yields to 6 tonnes per hectare, instead of 4 tonnes taken in the previous run. The results indicated that basic needs could be satisfied to the desired levels.

Table 10. Evolution of the main economic and demographic and health indicators for Asia.

	1960	1980	2000	2020	2040
Economic indicators					
GNP/capita	89.7	135.6	262.8	450.7	707.3
Investment rate (% *GNP*)	16	17	25	25	25
Consumption (% *GNP*)	49.7	58.16	52.28	48.06	47.93
% GNP allocated to food	27.2	18.94	15.70	21.20	22.27
Demographic and health indicators					
Population growth rate (%)	2.42	2.55	2.01	1.73	1.38
Total population (*millions*)	1544	2526	4021	5794	7940
Life expectancy (*years*)	48.6	55.65	66.8	66.17	66.72
Crude mortality rate	17.30	12.81	6.47	7.84	9.25
Infant mortality	148	99	32.2	33.8	32.4
Birthrate	37.8	37.1	25.55	24.9	22.7
Persons/family	4.63	4.92	4.69	4.27	3.56

Table 11. Evolution of the main economic and demographic and health indicators for Asia (second run).

	1960	1980	2000	2020	2040	2060
Economic indicators						
GNP/capita	89.72	135.6	267.5	506.2	928.8	1.516
Investment rate (% *of GNP*)	16	17	25	25	25	25
Consumption (% *of GNP*)	49.7	58.16	53.07	52.16	53.83	53.55
% of GNP allocated to food	27.2	18.94	15.25	14.70	12.84	13.73
Demographic and health indicators						
Population growth rate (%)	2.42	2.55	2.04	1.16	0.82	0.55
Total population (*millions*)	1544	2526	4025	5498	6701	7649
Life expectancy (*years*)	48.06	55.65	66.77	67.83	68.36	68.68
Crude mortality rate	17.30	12.81	6.54	7.26	9.80	12.16
Birthrate	37.79	37.09	25.84	18.79	18.04	17.58
Infant mortality	148	98.95	32.58	29.60	28.38	27.49
Persons/family	4.63	4.92	4.72	3.47	3.24	3.04

Per capita food consumption reaches 3000 calories in 1994, and 6 years later the required consumption of proteins is also achieved. School registration reaches 98% between 2000 and 2010, but the goal of one house per family is only reached in 2020.

The evolution of the most important economic variables is set out in Table 11. GNP per inhabitant — U.S. $89.70 in 1960 — reaches U.S. $506.20 in 2020, when all basic needs are satisfied, and is U.S. $1516 in 2060 (Table 11).

In spite of this considerable improvement, food is still a problem for the region. In the mid 2030s the remaining land has all been used although adequate food supplies are maintained until the end of the run. This is due to the existing reserves; the concentration on livestock and fisheries; and to the low population growth rate. In the last years of the run, however, the capacity to produce food is stretched to its limits, and it is inevitable that some years after 2060 Asia will not be able to feed its inhabitants adequately.

To solve the food problem in the long term, the region could adopt other measures. It could try to increase agricultural yields even further and produce food from nonconventional sources. These measures could be complemented with an effective family planning policy (with regard to the criteria set out in Chapter 5) to help close the gap between demographic growth and food production in the long term. There is sufficient time available before the crisis for an effective policy in both directions to be adopted.

Economic Growth

It is important to point out that economic growth rates for each year and for each region are, throughout the standard run, within the ranges considered "normal" at the present time. In underdeveloped regions, the growth rate in the 1960s and 1970s fluctuated around 4%; at the end of this century, and at the beginning of the next, there is an increase to over 5%, and in the case of Africa, to over 6%. Thereafter, there is a gradual decline, until average values of 3% are reached in the last years of the run.

The acceleration of economic growth toward the end of this century and beginning of the next is mainly due to two factors: an increased rate of investment, which goes from under 20 to 25%, and the effect of eliminating the negative balance-of-payments in foreign trade.

World Population

In Table 12 there is a comparison of population as calculated in the model with projections of the United Nations. To help interpret the figures in the table, the following points should be noted:

(a) Population values given by the model have been corrected to incorporate countries not included in the work (see Chapter 4); they total 32.4 million people. It is assumed that the population of those countries increases at the same rate as the population of the rest of the world.

(b) The low United Nations projection refers to developing countries only. For the developed countries, medium projections were taken.

Technological Progress and Socioeconomic Goals

The future of technological progress is currently a much debated subject. Positions vary greatly, ranging from those who maintain that technological progress will stop in the near future, to those who assume that it will continue more-or-less indefinitely, as it has in the recent past.

Given the importance of this issue, a run was carried out to test the effect on the evolution of the regions of technological progress ceasing in the relatively near future. For the computer run, it was assumed that the rate of technological progress used in the previous runs began to diminish from 1980, reaching zero in the year 2000. In other words, it is supposed that there is no more technological progress after the year 2000, and that returns to scale are constant. The result of this run, by regions, was as follows.

Developed Countries — Stopping technological progress does not have significant effects on basic needs; these are satisfied in the same period as in

Table 12. Comparison of world population as calculated by the model and the United Nations projections (in millions).

Year	Model	Average UN projection[a]	% difference with the model	Low UN projection[b]	% difference with the model
2000	6.419 (6.362)	6.513	−1.47%	5.977	+7.4%
2050	10.404 (10.311)	11.228	−7.34%	−	−

[a]*World Population Prospects as Assessed in 1968.* New York, United Nations, 1973, p. 63–65.
[b]*1974 World Population Year.* Special Edition. Geneva, ILO (the projection only goes to the year 2000).
Note: The figures in parentheses are those given by the model, without correction.

Table 13. Evolution of the main economic indicators for the developed countries. In this run it is assumed that there is no technological progress from the year 2000.

	1960	1980	2000	2020	2040	2060
GNP/capita	1402	2755	3966	5156	6291	7676
Investment rate (% *of GNP*)	20.60	23.16	29.14	28.11	32.9	39.85
Consumption (% *of GNP*)	49.50	57.17	54.68	58	56.48	53.47
% of GNP allocated to food	16.70	8.57	4.94	3.98	3.54	2.23

Table 14. Evolution of the main economic indicators for Latin America. In this run it is assumed that there is no technological progress from the year 2000.

	1960	1980	2000	2020	2040	2060
GNP/capita	371.8	498.1	688.7	901	1050	1173
Investment rate (% *of GNP*)	18.2	20.78	25	25	25	25
Consumption (% *of GNP*)	49.6	56.07	52.09	50.55	48.11	45.49
% of GNP allocated to food	21.20	14.31	11.63	8.42	4.95	8.67

the standard run, because the desired levels are reached before the rate of technological progress has declined significantly.

The consequences for general economic development, on the other hand, are very important (Table 13). The rate of investment increases smoothly, reaching 39.8% by 2060. The consumption sector, which in the standard run receives 80% of the GNP in 2060, receives only 53.47% for the same year. Per capita GNP — U.S. $7076 in 2060 — is also considerably less than in the standard run.

The high levels of investment result from the requirement that the per capita growth rate must be between 1 and 2%. Owing to the reduced rate of increase in productivity, the economic system needs to increase investment to achieve the minimum growth goal. Thus the restriction on the rate of investment (a maximum of 25% of GNP) must be relaxed; it has a lower priority than the rate of growth in the economy.

Latin America — The long-term consequences of a discontinuation of technological progress are far more serious for Latin America than for the developed countries. The basic needs can be satisfied, although only over a longer time period than in the standard run, particularly in the cases of food and housing.

The delay in satisfying basic needs also affects demographic evolution, although this effect is relatively small. The rate of population growth is somewhat greater than that registered in the standard run (0.58% in 2060 instead of 0.43%), which leads to a population of 856.3 million (compared with 759.2 million in the standard run).

It is in the general living conditions that the effect of a reduced rate in technological progress is more noticeable (Table 14). GNP per capita, which reached U.S. $5746 in 2060 in the standard run, is reduced to U.S. $1173 for the same year. The proportion of GNP devoted to consumer goods and services remains at a low level throughout the run, and amounts to 45.49% by 2060; this is practically the minimum level allowed.

In this run the rate of investment does not exceed 25%, and the reduction in the GNP per capita is far more marked than for the developed countries. Here is a conflict between two of the restrictions for developing countries that were described at the beginning of this chapter.

The first is that, once the satisfaction of basic needs has been achieved, education and housing improve at a preestablished rate with the increased investment they receive. The second is that GNP per capita must grow at a minimum rate of 2% per annum. To comply with this second restriction, the rate of investment must exceed the upper limit of 25%, owing to the stagnation in productivity. With the slow growth of the economy, this would reduce investment in basic needs; as these have priority over economic growth, the optimization violates the restriction concerning minimum growth and investment does not increase beyond the preestablished maximum.

Latin America can therefore satisfy its basic needs within a reasonable period, but this would entail keeping the other elements of well-being at minimum levels.

Africa — In Africa, as in Asia, the minimum objectives cannot be achieved if technological progress stops; the economic system finally collapses.

Of the basic needs, only food reaches the target level, and then only for a brief period. Housing reaches a maximum of 0.51 houses per family in 2012, only to decline from then on. School registrations for basic education reach a maximum of 70% in 2014, and then decline for the rest of the run (Fig. 23).

The demographic evolution clearly reflects the deficiencies in meeting basic needs. The rate of population growth is maintained at approximately its 1970 level of 2.6%. Thus the population grows rapidly, increasing by 6.6-fold by the year 2032 (to 1707 million), whereas in the standard run it only increased 5-fold by 2060 (1260 million).

In Table 15 and Fig. 23 the evolution of the principal economic and demographic and health indicators is shown. The run was stopped in the year 2032 for the reasons already given for the case of Asia in the standard run.

The economic indicators illustrate how the production system almost collapses. Owing to the effort needed to raise the level of production to that corresponding to the satisfaction of the basic needs, the rate of saving, after

97

FIGURE 23

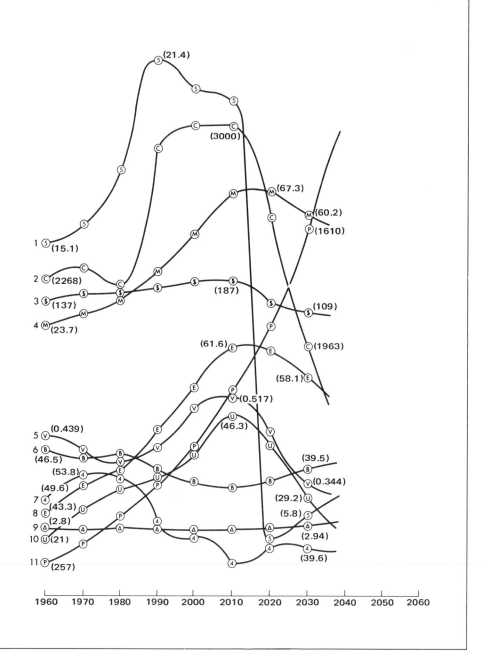

reaching 23% in 1986, is progressively reduced until it reaches values below those considered acceptable. At the same time, the percentage of GNP allocated to the food sector increases from 26.4% in 1960 to 41.1% in 2030. In the standard run, the proportion of GNP allocated to food was only 9.7% in 2030.

The GNP per capita grows slowly and reaches a maximum of U.S. $189 in 2006; it then begins to decrease even though total GNP continues to increase slowly, since the population increases rapidly.

The main cause of the collapse is the rapid population growth, which stems from the delay in raising the level of satisfaction of basic needs in the first decades of the run. As the population grows, it becomes increasingly more difficult to raise this level, and this, in turn, maintains the high rate of population growth.

In a real situation, the process would obviously be different. Society would concentrate all its economic efforts on the production of food to maintain the population at a minimum level of activity, and on the preservation of the most important infrastructural services; investments in all other areas of social interest — housing, education, health, etc. — would be reduced. The result would be a society where the majority of the population would be uneducated and subject to great suffering, subsisting on food levels only just over the minimum necessary for survival. This is the situation that currently exists in many countries of the Third World. The most important difference between this and the "ideal" situation is that, as in current societies, high levels of consumption would be preserved for the minorities with the political and economic power.

The main conclusion derived from the model is the warning that, if technological progress is stopped, it would be impossible for Africa to achieve the socioeconomic objectives proposed in this study, even if the total collapse predicted by the run does not materialize.

Asia — The evolution of Asia, assuming that technological progress stops, is very similar to that of Africa, with the difference that none of the basic needs reaches the proposed levels.

Population increases rapidly, and the demographic indicators behave similarly to those of Africa. The causes of economic collapse are also similar (see Table 16 and Fig. 24).

In conclusion, the runs show that, for the countries of the Third World, continued technological progress is essential if they are to be liberated from underdevelopment and misery. This does not mean that technological progress should continue along the same lines as in the past; indeed, these have largely contributed to widening the gap that separates the rich sectors from the poor sectors of humanity.

Fig. 23. Time period and conditions required for Africa to satisfy basic needs to given levels, assuming that there is no technological progress beyond 2000.

1 Percentage of GNP allocated to sector 5 (5)	7 Percentage of GNP allocated to sector 4 (4)
2 Total calories (C)	8 Life expectancy (E)
3 GNP per capita in 1960 dollars ($)	9 Population growth rate ($\triangle$)
4 Enrollment (M)	10 Urbanization (U)
5 Houses per family (V)	11 Total population (P)
6 Birthrate (B)	

Table 15. Evolution of the main economic and demographic and health indicators for Africa. In this run it is assumed that there is no technological progress beyond the year 2000.

	1960	1980	2000	2010	2020	2030
Economic indicators						
GNP/capita	136.9	157.3	184.4	186.7	133	109.8
Investment rate (% *of GNP*)	15.1	16.47	20.36	20.01	5.02	5.08
Consumption (% *of GNP*)	49.6	53.76	42.44	36.8	40	39.5
% of GNP allocated to food	26.4	22.3	20.95	21.34	27.63	43
Demographic and health indicators						
Rate of population growth (%)	2.46	2.72	2.56	2.55	2.73	2.94
Total population (*millions*)	257	432.8	728.1	938	1212	1610
Life expectancy (*years*)	43.3	48	57	61.6	61.1	58.1
Crude mortality rate	20.6	17.37	10.8	8.27	8.54	10.25
Birthrate	46.54	43.48	35.30	33	35.66	39.45
Infant mortality	196	166.3	83.79	45.82	45.54	66.17
Persons/family	4.46	4.71	4.91	5.04	5.21	5.35

International Solidarity

As has already been seen, all the regions into which the world has been divided could, by their own efforts, eventually reach the levels of satisfaction of basic needs proposed in this work.

However, the conditions under which each region could achieve these objectives differ. The developed countries, together with Latin America, can achieve them more easily and rapidly than Asia and Africa and, more importantly, can aspire to levels of general well-being that are very much higher, as indicated by the final levels of per capita income and by the proportion of GNP allocated to consumer goods and services.

An obvious way of eliminating or reducing these inequalities is through international cooperation. To test the effects that international cooperation might have, a run was made incorporating the following assumptions:

(a) the developed countries allocate 2% of their GNP to economic aid. This aid would take the form of net transfer of capital, without a commitment to repay;

(b) the aid is devoted exclusively to Asia and Africa, the most needy regions;

(c) the distribution of the aid to those regions is directly proportional to their populations and inversely proportional to life expectancy at birth; this distribution is calculated every year, and therefore varies throughout the run;

(d) capital transfer begins in 1980, at the level of 0.2% of GNP of the industrialized countries; it increases by 0.2% of GNP per year, until it reaches 2% in 1990. Once the satisfaction of basic needs within one region has been achieved, aid begins to diminish at the same rate of 0.2% of the donor's country GNP, and thus ceases completely after 10 years.

The results of this run, by region, are given below.

Developed Countries — The rate of economic growth of the developed

Table 16. Evolution of the main economic and demographic and health indicators for Asia. In this run it is assumed that there is no technological progress beyond the year 2000.

	1960	1980	2000	2010	2020	2030
Economic indicators						
GNP/capita	89.7	126.5	150.5	153.1	114	89.23
Investment rate (% of GNP)	16	16.63	25	23.64	10.72	6.39
Consumption (% of GNP)	49.7	57.66	48.62	44.15	42.56	36.06
% of GNP allocated to agriculture	27.2	19.59	17.66	21.12	32.13	45.1
Demographic and health indicators						
Population growth rate (%)	2.42	2.58	2.52	2.36	2.37	2.48
Total population (*millions*)	1544	2529	4230	5383	6784	8633
Life expectancy (*years*)	48.06	55.07	64.11	65.9	65.8	65.2
Crude mortality rate	17.3	13.11	7.51	6.72	7.12	7.7
Infant mortality	148	102.7	39.83	34.27	34.48	35.68
Birthrate	37.8	37.87	31.68	29.61	30.65	32.57
Persons/family	4.63	4.94	5.12	5.07	5.08	5.27

countries is higher than in the standard run, although it never surpasses the upper limit of 2%. Per capita production in 2060 amounts to U.S. $14 250, compared with U.S. $9670 in the standard run.

The higher rate of economic growth is due to a reaction of the economy — produced by the interplay of the constraints — to the drainage of capital caused by the aid. It has to be remembered that to limit the economic growth of the developed countries between 1 and 2% assumes a political decision, as the capacity of growth of the bloc is much higher. In a real situation, therefore, the developed bloc can help the other countries without necessarily increasing their rate of economic growth, or increasing it only in the required amount to compensate for the aid. We did not attempt to tighten the constraint on growth, because it is maintained within the allowed interval, and because the run shows that the aid is not decisive for the developing countries, even if its absolute amount is greater than the one possible in the standard run.

Basic needs are satisfied in the same period as before, and the health and demographic variables are maintained at practically the same levels.

The rate of investment is higher than in the standard run (15.78% in 2060), corresponding to the higher rate of economic growth. There is very little variation in the other economic indicators, although the general level of well-being is improved.

Africa — Aid does not affect the time periods within which basic needs are satisfied, with the exception of housing; this is because nearly all the basic needs reach high levels in the standard run before aid has much influence.

The limited effect of aid on the time period required to satisfy basic needs suggests that demographic variables would not be greatly affected. The rate of population growth is somewhat lower, and, as a result, population in the year 2060 — 1160 million — is 8% lower than on the standard run. Life expectancy and infant mortality are practically unchanged.

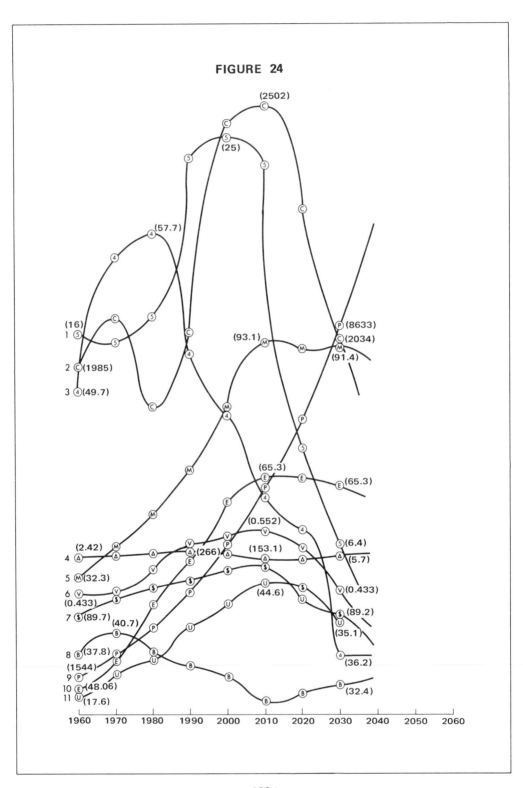

FIGURE 24

The greatest effects of aid are felt in the first decades of the next century, and are shown particularly in a per capita income that is considerably higher than in the standard run. This increase — to 142% of the standard run value in 2000, and 122% of the value for that run in 2060 — makes a better level of general well-being possible, as can be seen from the increase in other services and consumer goods. Additionally, it leads to improved provision for basic needs, particularly education and housing.

Asia — The effect of aid on Asia is similar to that on Africa; the only basic need affected is housing, which now achieves the desired levels about 15 years earlier than in the standard run. Demographic indicators are little affected. The final population of the region in 2060 is 15% less than in the standard run.

The greatest difference between Asia and Africa appears in the economic indicators. The increase in production is of the same magnitude as in Africa, but consumption remains more or less the same. This is due to the fact that, in the standard run the levels of education and housing in Asia are inferior to those in Africa. Therefore, Asia must devote a greater proportion of her income than Africa to the improvement of these basic services.

The Satisfaction of Basic Needs and Income Distribution

The model proposes that everyone should have equal access to those goods necessary for the satisfaction of basic needs; equality of opportunity for those goods and services not included in these needs is also advocated. In other words, an essentially egalitarian income distribution is assumed.

Some maintain, however, that an adequate level of well-being could be achieved for the entire population by encouraging economic growth, without resorting to drastic modification in income distribution. According to this argument, the whole level of the economy must be raised before income is transferred from the richer sectors to the poorer sectors of the population.

The egalitarian assumption of the model is based more on a sense of basic justice and social solidarity than on technical economic considerations. However, it is worth comparing the two positions in terms of economic feasibility.

Calculations were made to establish the average GNP per capita that would be necessary for the basic needs of each person to be satisfied, on the assumption that the current income structure is maintained for the countries considered. Table 17 shows the income distribution in the world before 1965, classifying countries according to GNP per capita. For the purposes of this table, populations are categorized according to income. Each of the first four

---

Fig. 24. Time period and conditions required for Asia to satisfy basic needs to given levels, assuming that there is no technological progress beyond 2000.

1 Percentage of GNP allocated to sector 5 (5)
2 Total calories (C)
3 Percentage of GNP allocated to sector 4 (4)
4 Population growth rate (△)
5 Enrollment (M)
6 Houses per family (V)

7 GNP per capita in 1960 dollars ($)
8 Birthrate (B)
9 Total population (P)
10 Life expectancy at birth (E)
11 Urbanization (U)

Table 17. Indicators of income distribution in the year 1965 (approximate).

GNP/capita	No. countries	Q_1	Q_2	Q_3	Q_4	P_{80-95}	P_{96-100}
		Percentages					
Less than 100	9	7.0	10.0	13.1	19.4	21.4	29.1
101–200	8	5.3	8.6	12.0	17.5	31.6	24.9
201–300	11	4.8	8.0	11.3	18.1	25.7	32.0
301–500	9	4.5	7.9	12.3	18.0	27.4	30.0
501–1000	6	5.1	8.9	13.9	22.1	24.7	25.4
1001–2000	10	4.7	10.5	15.9	22.2	25.7	20.9
2001 and over	3	5.0	10.9	17.9	24.1	26.3	16.4

Note: Q_1 represents total personal income received by the poorest 20%; Q_2, that of the next 20%, etc.; P_{96-100} is the share of the richest 5%; P_{80-95} is that of the next 15%.

Source: Paukert, F. *Income distribution at different levels of development: a survey of evidence.* International Labour Review, 108 (2-3), Aug/Sep 1973.

categories comprises 20% of the population; the fifth comprises 15%, and the last contains the most privileged 5%.

Income is expressed as the percentage of production accruing to each category.

The calculation was made on the basis of the following premises:
(a) it is considered that the basic needs of all inhabitants are satisfied when the least privileged 20% reaches an income level permitting fulfillment of these needs;
(b) the minimum income level — or GNP per capita — necessary to satisfy basic needs is calculated on the basis of the assumptions made for the standard run of the model.

Calculations were made for the 15 regions into which the world is divided in the model built by V. Leontief for the United Nations[11] (exluding the People's Republic of China because of lack of income distribution data). This regionalization was preferred because it includes more homogeneous groups of countries than the regions into which the world is divided for the present work. The model was run for each of the regions to establish the minimum GNP required to satisfy basic needs. The results of these runs appear in Table 18. As can be seen, in the underdeveloped countries, the GNP per capita needed to satisfy basic needs in egalitarian conditions is something between three and five times less than that required if current income structures are maintained. Even in capitalist countries, this factor varies between 2.6 for Japan and 4.3 for the most advanced Western European countries. Only in socialist states, where income distribution is more egalitarian, is the factor lower than 2.[12]

---

[11]The regions used were taken from the model of the world economy of the United Nations, based on V. Leontief, *Structure of the world economy.* American Economic Review, 64(6), Dec 1974. Calculations were made in Geneva by the ILO by M. Hopkins and H. D. Scolnik, with collaboration from M. McLean, in May and June 1975.

[12]Data on income distribution in the socialist countries and other complementary data on other regions were taken from S. Jain and A. Tieman, *Size distribution of income: a compilation of data.* Washington, D.C., World Bank, Development Research Centre Discussion Paper No. 4, 1973 (Mimeo.).

Table 18. Results of runs of the model to establish the minimum GNP required to satisfy basic needs.

Regions[a]	A Proportion of total income received by the poorest 20% (% of GNP)	B GNP per capita required to satisfy basic needs with egalitarian income distribution	C GNP per capita required to satisfy basic needs if the present income distribution is maintained	$\frac{C}{B}$
North America	5.7	4407	15463	3.5
South America (more developed)	4.0	807	4035	5
South America (less developed)	4.1	740	3610	4.9
Western Europe (more developed)	4.6	2164	9409	4.3
Western Europe (less developed)	5.3	892	3366	3.8
USSR	10.4	1602	3081	1.9
Eastern Europe	10.4	1359	2613	1.9
Japan	7.7	2416	6275	2.6
Far East and India	7.3	428	1173	2.7
Middle East (oil-producing states)	5.6	540	1929	3.6
Africa (more developed)	5.5	451	1640	3.6
Africa (less developed)	4.8	505	2104	4.1
South Africa	1.9	1093	11505	10.1
Australia and New Zealand	7.0	2867	8191	2.8
People's Republic of China	No data	—	—	—

[a]Regions from model of the world economy of the United Nations (see footnote 11).

With these results, a comparison can be made of the social and economic consequences of the two growth hypotheses considered.

First, to maintain the current income structures would considerably prolong the time required to satisfy the basic needs of the population. The extent of this delay can be evaluated from the standard run of the model, particularly for Africa and Latin America, where Leontief's regions approximately coincide with those used in this work (although the values of GNP per capita are somewhat different because the regions do not coincide exactly). Income distribution is practically the same in both approaches in the regions, and therefore the multiplying factor in the table can be applied approximately to the results of the model.

In Africa, as has already been seen, basic needs are satisfied in the model around the year 2008, with an average income per capita of U.S. $558. If it is supposed that the current structure of income is maintained, it can be seen

Table 19. Economic growth rates necessary to satisfy basic needs in the year 2000, maintaining the current income distribution structure.

	Growth rates in the period 1960–70	Growth rates necessary to satisfy basic needs in the year 2000
North America	4.5	5.3
South America (more developed)	5.3	9.9
South America (less developed)	5.2	10.5
Western Europe (more developed)	4.6	5.7
Western Europe (less developed)	6.7	7.9
USSR	7.0	4.1
Eastern Europe	5.7	3.4
Japan	10.6	5.9
Far East and India	5.3	10.5
Middle East (oil-producing states)	8.5	10.4
Africa (more developed)	4.1	11.5
Africa (less developed)	5.1	11.8
South Africa	6.0	12.8
Australia and New Zealand	4.9	5.6
People's Republic of China	4.4	No data

from the multiplying factor in Table 19 that this income should increase to U.S. $2000 if the same level of satisfaction is to be achieved. The value is only reached in the model in the year 2046, 38 years later than with the first hypothesis. In Latin America, basic needs can be satisfied in the year 1992 with an income per capita of U.S. $809, but the value of U.S. $4045, considered necessary by the second hypothesis, is only reached in 2043 — approximately 50 years later. Both examples are sufficient to illustrate what would happen in other regions of the world.

To show the magnitude of the problem in another way, the economic growth rates that would be necessary for the population of all the countries in the world to achieve satisfaction of basic needs have been calculated assuming it were to take approximately the same time periods as the standard run of the model, and maintaining the current structure of income (Table 19). As can be seen, the growth rates of the underdeveloped countries should be between 10 and 12%.

In summary, it can be said that economic growth with the preservation of the current income distribution system would, at the very best, delay the goal of a liberated humanity, free from suffering and misery, by at least two generations. It also implies the need to devote between three and five times more material resources to the achievement of the desired objective, thus multiplying the pressure on the environment, and all this to maintain the careless consumption of privileged minorities.

Conclusion

The results of the model set out in the previous chapter demonstrate that, if the policies proposed here are applied, all of humanity could attain an adequate standard of living within a period a little longer than one generation. The satisfaction of the most essential physical and cultural needs, which has been one of the central objectives of man from his beginnings, could be fulfilled for most of the countries of the Third World toward the end of the century, or in the first years of the next.

The only problem of physical limitation that arises, and which is of a local nature, is the exhaustion of the supply of cultivatable land in Asia in the middle of the next century. However, the large reserves of cultivatable land in other regions could easily cover this deficit. Since the effects of this limitation would only begin to be felt in 80 years, Asia has enough time to look for its own solutions to the problem, such as increasing the yield of crops, which has been assumed to be well below the theoretically possible levels; producing food from nonconventional sources; the application of an effective family planning policy that would enable the population to achieve a balance within a shorter period than predicted by the model; etc.

The model also shows that it is possible to control population growth to the point of equilibrium by raising the general standard of living, particularly with relation to basic needs. This equilibrium could be achieved on a global scale well before the earth's capacity to produce food — the only foreseeable physical limitation within the time horizon of the model — is fully exploited, even if food production continues to be based on currently available technology.

The obstacles that currently stand in the way of the harmonious development of humanity are not physical or economic in the strict sense, but essentially sociopolitical. In effect, the growth rates with which the desired objectives are achieved are, as was seen in the previous chapter, those considered normal in the current economic situation. The goals are therefore achieved not by very high economic growth, but by a reduction in nonessential consumption; increased investment; the elimination of socioeconomic and political barriers, which currently hinder the rational use of land, both for food production and for urban planning; the egalitarian distribution of basic goods and services; and, in developing countries, the implementation of an active policy to eliminate deficits in international trade.

The growth rates necessary to achieve these objectives, and which can be easily attained without imposing intolerable social sacrifice, contrast with those required to satisfy, in approximately the same period of time, the basic needs within the current income structure, or the same socioeconomic organization. These economic growth rates, which for developing countries vary between 10 and nearly 12%, are in fact impossible to attain, for the reasons set out in the previous section. To propose this type of "solution,"

107

therefore, is only to propose a preservation of the current status quo and to misunderstand the true causes of the crisis that currently affects the world.

One of the most interesting results of the model is the light it sheds on the effect that possible international aid, in particular the transfer of resources from the industrialized countries to the poor countries, would have. Even if a greater level of international aid than that advised by the United Nations is implemented, it may contribute to raise the level of well-being at the time of transfer, but in no way decisively. What has been seen with regard to income distribution clearly demonstrates that international aid, in the conditions currently prevailing in most developing countries, would only contribute to increasing spending by privileged sectors, and would have little or no effect on the living conditions of the majority of the population. The effect of the transfer of capital is only significant for the general well-being if there are conditions of social equality similar to those proposed in the model.

International solidarity can take forms other than the net transfer of resources from rich to poor countries. The model shows the recovery that developing countries can achieve in economic growth precisely at the decisive stage of attaining the satisfaction of basic needs, through the elimination of a negative balance of payments. The developed countries can help to bring forward the attainment of this objective by fixing fair prices for the products of underdeveloped countries to replace present prices that, rather than representing a just distribution between the factors of production of the two production sectors into which the world is divided, are the consequence of an unequal distribution of economic, political, and military power. Moreover, with a reduction in their growth rates, as proposed in the model, the rich countries could contribute to relieving the pressure on available resources, helping the poor countries indirectly in this way.

In the previous chapter, it was shown that in the year 2060 (at which the computer runs were terminated) there would still be inequalities, expressed in economic indicators, between the levels of well-being in the developed and poor countries, particularly with respect to Asia. To evaluate correctly the significance of this remaining gap, it should be borne in mind that the results of the model over such a long period of time could change considerably with relatively small fluctuations in some of the variables used; a moderate increase in the rate of technological progress, for example, could easily close the gap.

Lastly the model shows, within the obvious limitations of this type of work, that the fate of man does not depend, in the last instance, on insurmountable physical barriers but on social and political factors that man must modify. Their solution is not at all easy, because to change the organization and values of society, as history has shown, is much more difficult than overcoming physical limitations. To attempt the task, however, is the only way open to an improved humanity.

It could possibly be said that this proposal is utopian, and that it would be more realistic to propose solutions that involve less radical modifications to the sociopolitical structure of the world. Those who hold this position should be reminded of the words of John Stuart Mill more than a century ago:

> *"For a great evil, a small remedy does not produce a small result; it*
> *simply does not produce any results at all."*